Strategy and Training

The *Meaningful Ambitions Initiative*

All the royalties from this book are donated to the *Meaningful Ambitions* benevolent society (called *Energie Jeunes* in France).

Meaningful Ambitions uses training methods employed in the business world to prevent young people from dropping out of education. It organises educational initiatives for underprivileged teenagers in junior high schools, with the support of corporate partners such as Air Liquide, Atos, Axa, Korda & Partners, L'Oréal, Orange, SMABTP, Spie Batignolles and Verlingue.

Thanks to dozens of businesspeople freely giving their time, thousands of young people have already found the inner motivation to help them avoid the slippery slope to failure.

Further information is available on-line at www.meaningfulambitions.com

To contact the author: philippe.korda@korda-partners.com

Strategy and Training

Making Skills a Competitive Advantage

Philippe Korda

business**expert**
Press

Strategy and Training: Making Skills a Competitive Advantage
Copyright © Business Expert Press, 2012.

First published in 2012 by
Business Expert Press, LLC
222 East 46th Street, New York, NY 10017
www.businessexpertpress.com

ISBN-13: 978-1-60649-572-8 (paperback)

ISBN-13: 978-1-60649-573-5 (e-book)

DOI 10.4128/9781606495735

Business Expert Press Strategic Management collection

Collection ISSN: 2150-9611 (print)
Collection ISSN: 2150-9646 (electronic)

Cover design by Jonathan Pennell
Interior design by Exeter Premedia Services Private Ltd.,
Chennai, India

First edition: 2012

10 9 8 7 6 5 4 3 2 1

Printed in the United States of America.

Abstract

This book explores corporate training in the context of deploying strategic initiatives within organisations. It goes beyond merely explaining strategy, to investigating how it relates to skills training, and how companies can leverage this to implement their initiatives.

Drawing on real-life client examples and the inspirational stories of highly successful individuals, this book highlights approaches that have transformed organisations and re-invented training. It dispels myths that exist around traditional training paradigms and brings to light the effectiveness of new methods and approaches.

Social learning, using technologies such as Twitter and video-blogs, is today revolutionising the way training is undertaken. At the same time, the age-old communication technique of storytelling is being reinvented as a way to roll out strategic programs to large multi-cultural groups on a global scale. The author presents key questions that are relevant at project and company level, and provide practical checklists and summaries complementing each chapter of the book.

This text highlights how you can develop your team's expertise through systematic coaching when cascading a strategy throughout your organisation, and explains the benefits of reinforcing strengths, identifying weaknesses and correcting failures to build competitive advantage. It also addresses the risk of 'unlearning' post-training, and issues that arise with maintaining performance evaluation and measuring tangible progress.

Succinct and pragmatic, the book reveals how strategic projects can be successfully rolled out globally, using cost-effective training that will ensure a return on investment for your organisation.

Keywords

strategy, strategic programs, training, training models, skills development, practical tools, social learning

Contents

Introduction

This book had its origins in two ideas. The first was the realization that most strategic projects fail. The second was the belief that training can now establish a new order. Various studies have demonstrated that only two out of five strategic projects succeed in delivering the anticipated results on time and budget. That is an enormous waste, and improved training can improve the success rate of new strategic initiatives.

It goes without saying that not all strategies are intrinsically wrong. Using *innovation* to stand out from the crowd: not a bad idea, on paper. Providing *solutions* rather than mere products: that should be of interest to customers. Transforming your *economic model* and drastically reducing your cost structure to dominate existing markets or create the markets of the future: that sounds promising, in principle. The list could go on.

No, when strategies fail it is mainly due to defects in their *execution*, that is to say, in *people's inability to implement the strategy effectively*. In more than half of all cases, failure is connected to the difficulty of changing priorities, working methods, and patterns of behavior quickly enough within an organization—including the everyday habits of employees in direct contact with the product or customer.

For example, a strategy based on innovation can only succeed if employees are really capable, as a group, of doing better than the competition at generating, developing, bringing to market, and selling new products or services. Meanwhile, a strategy based on quality of service can only prove successful if your entire workforce is able to provide flawless service throughout the customer relationship process.

The problem is even more immediate in moving from *strategy* per se to the major *action plans* through which it is implemented: successfully launching a new and innovative product, making beneficial changes to your organization, fully implementing and using a new IT system, and so on. These all require staff with a great ability to do *new* things and to do things *differently*.

It would therefore be tempting to say: "Most strategies fail *because not enough employees are sufficiently skilled to implement them effectively.*" However, this would be incorrect and unfair, because a good strategy takes proper account of employees' skills.

Let us imagine that a senior manager heading an underqualified and inexperienced workforce formulated a strategy so sophisticated and difficult to implement that his employees were doomed to fail. Who would be responsible for that disaster? If it were a General, planning a military campaign, or a football manager preparing for the cup final, we would quickly know where to lay the blame.

The fact remains that skills "existing" at a particular time are rarely sufficient to achieve a great ambition. What counts, when drawing up a strategy, is the workforce's *potential* and the resources at the business's disposal to exploit that potential. That is why training is absolutely essential.

So why, currently, is training so underused as a tool for implementing strategy? It is this specific aspect of training, and this alone, that we address in this book. The publication is neither a general training manual nor a summary of educational methods. Rather, it is a work on strategy that focuses on training as a means of deployment. This aspect is critical, given that training is constantly changing due to the ongoing technological revolution.

No one has a miracle solution when it comes to using training to implement strategy. Every business is different, every strategy is unique, and everything can change very quickly. This book does not hand down lessons in tablets of stone but it offers senior business people and training professionals some nuggets of wisdom, drawn from authoritative data, together with recommendations for action supported by specific examples.

The first subject to be addressed concerns *purpose*: Exactly what is the purpose of training from a strategic perspective? Looking beyond its philosophical nature, there are some very practical aspects to this question. The usual response is that the purpose of training is to develop *skills*. We shall endeavor to demonstrate that such thinking is no longer really sufficient in the world in which we live. The book also questions a number of widely held assumptions about the *way* in which training should be carried out.

The first chapter highlights the need to assign new roles of training, roles directly connected to strategy. It suggests a new definition for the objectives of major business training programs. The second chapter argues for a thorough transformation of the training methods employed in strategy implementation plans. Up-to-date findings of extensive scientific research suggest most existing teaching practices actually get in the way of achieving excellence. Fortunately, we shall discover solutions that have proven effective for business strategy training.

The third chapter questions the current tendency to see only weaknesses in organizations and individuals, and to systematically resort to skills standards in an attempt to enforce uniform practices and behavior. It proposes a "situational" approach to training, suggesting that the training process should be designed differently depending on the challenge it is addressing. The appropriate choice might involve introducing new activities, correcting competitive weaknesses or making better use of the business's strengths. Likewise, training must take a quite different approach to each individual, depending on their situation and the skill required.

The fourth chapter recommends that employees undergoing training should be viewed as capable human beings who can resolve problems (not merely apply solutions), display emotional intelligence, and take initiatives. This assumes that training takes account of various skills required to implement a strategy, the different ways of learning, and the need to employ "universal languages."

The fifth chapter argues for training in strategic issues to take full advantage of new opportunities provided by the collaborative tools and systems of Web 2.0: social networks, blogs and forums, to name a few. These open training up to new wide-ranging areas that are instantly accessible.

The sixth chapter invites the reader to review the principles of the past, which too often still determine the way in which we design and carry out training programs. Many old beliefs, such as those relating to optimum training group size or the role of the group leader, must now be challenged in the light of extensive and convincing experience.

The final part of the book is devoted to the *strategic economic management* of training. The seventh chapter recommends strategic training management, both in allocating human and financial resources and in measuring effectiveness. It demonstrates that real breakthroughs can be made in how strategic contribution of a training relates to the resources it consumes. The conclusion then asks the reader to reflect on assumptions about the development of training as a tool for strategy implementation over the years to come.

Each chapter has a similar structure. It opens with a business story presenting the issue, usually based on a real-life example. It concludes with a brief summary of the key points to remember and an important checklist of recommendations.

This book is the fruit of many years of experience supporting businesses that are at the cutting edge of deploying their strategies on every continent. It also includes the results of various international benchmarking studies conducted by Korda & Partners' teams on issues connected to training and strategy. The text draws on the academic work of outstanding researchers in disciplines as diverse as educational science, social psychology, thought-leading insights, and new technology. These experts are all credited and their most prominent or most recent works are listed at the end of the book.

CHAPTER 1

When Strategy Met Training

As an Era Ends, Another Begins

Strategy was an intelligent and friendly person, but a little bit of a control freak.

Teeming with ideas, she sometimes lost herself in abstract reflection but always came up with big exciting projects in the end. Unfortunately, she then struggled to follow them through in practice.

If the truth be told, she sometimes wondered who she really was, given the extent to which her name was misused and bandied about by senior managers.

She usually found herself teamed with *Finance*, *Budget*, *Reporting*, *Organization*, and *Information Systems*. She did not know *Training* very well yet and was still blissfully unaware of how her meeting with him would turn her life upside down.

Training was generous and hard working by nature, even if some thought him a little overidealistic.

He believed in people's ability to learn and develop. He was attentive to the expectations of senior executives, middle managers, and colleagues.

He devoted a lot of time to managing skills-development programs in every possible field.

Yet every year he also had to fight for his budget. Cruel people around him often reminded him that, even though held in high esteem, his work was costly and ultimately yielded few tangible benefits.

He was yet to discover how his encounter with *Strategy* would lighten up his life and give new meaning to his existence.

Over the course of this chapter, you will discover …

… just what strategy involves

In business and in the media, the word "strategy" is used so frequently and in so many different senses that it is useful for us to define its true meaning. Specialists in strategy can therefore skip the first part of this chapter.

… just what strategy now expects of training

We have moved on from the days when training merely served to create the skills required for an activity. Training faces new expectations; it is the target of growing criticism and yet, by developing a closer relationship with strategy, it is undergoing a revolution.

What Is a Strategy?

These days, "strategy" is one of the most widely used words in the business world: "strategic vision," "industrial strategy," "product strategy," "commercial strategy," "social strategy," "financial strategy," "purchasing strategy," "partnership strategy," "strategic initiatives"; the list is endless.

According to the *Shorter Oxford English Dictionary*, the word originates from Greek *stratêgia* and Latin *strategia*, and means "The art of a commander-in-chief; the planning and direction of the larger military movements and overall operations of a campaign" or, in a wider sense, "the art or skill of careful planning towards an advantage or a desired end."

Unlike tactics, which are local and time limited in scope (winning a battle), strategy relates to a longer-term general objective (winning the war).

Any organization facing enemies (or any other problem) must make it a priority to rely on a solid *strategy* to achieve the goals that have been set.

However, in the business world, many top executives use strategy to describe concepts that are actually quite different in nature.

Some of them refer to a corporation's *general mission*.

For example, "our strategy consists in helping to cure all the sick through a continually improving range of medication" or "our strategy is to supply safe, high-quality, environmentally friendly cars which are affordable by as many customers as possible."

All these declarations are useful and even praiseworthy, generally speaking. However, in no way do they show *how* the organization is going to gather its forces to achieve its objectives.

Other senior executives wrongly believe they refer to *strategy* when defining their organization's statistical objectives. For example, "our strategy is to achieve a 20% market share and to double in size within 5 years."

It is of course essential to clarify your goals. For example, when Boeing stopped trying to "be the world's leading aircraft maker" in favor of "being the world's most profitable aircraft maker," it marked a turning point for the company.

Yet having a strategy involves going further and defining *how* you will go about achieving your goals. In a competitive world, this requires you to establish, among other things, a *sustainable competitive advantage*.

Michael Porter, probably the world's acknowledged expert on the subject for the past 30 years, believes that there are only three types of strategy that can create that competitive advantage: cost leadership, differentiation, and focus.

Once we have clarified precisely what these terms mean, we shall see that we need to add a few concepts to define our subject more completely: "Blue Ocean" strategies, combining activities, strategic hierarchies, and strategic initiatives. In this way, we shall see what training can bring to strategy.

Cost-Leadership Strategies

For Ryanair, business has been booming despite the crisis in air travel. By 2010, it was already carrying as many passengers as Air France KLM and it could soon overtake Lufthansa to become Europe's leading airline.

The airline's phenomenal success has certainly raised eyebrows.

Not that this has anything at all to do with the benefits that it offers its employees: its pay levels are below the market rate, often circumvents social legislation, provides deplorable working conditions, and has even been heavily criticized by Amnesty International.

Neither is its success explained by the level of service offered to passengers. In every area, this is pared back to the minimum, and sometimes even less than the minimum!

Aggressive, provocative, and not afraid to speak his mind, its CEO Michael O'Leary never hesitates to publicly put customers in their place: "Our customer services department never answers emails. If you don't like it, you can go elsewhere! We never give refunds, whatever the reason. We don't fall for the 'My granny fell ill' excuse. And don't give us your sob stories—we're not interested. Queue at the check-in too long and you missed your flight? Tough! You're not happy? Take your custom elsewhere!"

Nor can Ryanair's success be credited to an environmentally friendly approach, as O'Leary specifically declared that "the best thing we can do with environmentalists is shoot them."[1]

What explains Ryanair's triumph is its cost-leadership strategy, which involves building an ultracompetitive economic model.

It goes without saying that a company benefiting structurally from lower costs than its competitors possesses two major assets: it can offer attractive prices to win a large number of customers, while dissuading its competitors from launching price wars that, by definition, they could never win.

A company adopting such a strategy is implicitly making several fundamental choices. Firstly, to focus on the mass market, to the exclusion of more sophisticated and demanding customers, who are bound to cost more to satisfy. Secondly, it is targeting high-volume business in order to achieve economies of scale. Lastly, it is opting to standardize its products and services as much as possible.

At Ryanair, the quest for savings is a clear obsession in every area. The corporation obliges local authorities to bear a proportion of its infrastructure costs. O'Leary prohibits his employees from recharging their mobile phones in the office to cut electricity bills—and O'Leary himself makes a point of only using free pens taken from hotel bedrooms.

Ryanair explicitly targets those customers who wish to travel at the lowest possible price and have no interest in any other services that are usually offered inby other airlines.

In a different era—and mercifully adopting a more customer-friendly style—corporations such as Kodak and IKEA succeeded in capturing markets by designing, manufacturing, and mass distributing simple, affordable, standardized products that met most consumers' expectations.

Differentiation Strategies

In the car industry, BMW has always taken the utmost care to *differentiate itself* from its competitors. It pays constant attention to its products, services, and brand image to ensure that the consumer willingly accepts the BMW's higher price compared with a similar model from other manufacturers.

To take other, very different examples, Apple has always differentiated itself on the basis of innovation and design, Amazon upon the customization of the advice provided, and Starbucks upon the ambiance of its coffee bars.

Those four businesses illustrate the *differentiation* strategy. Unlike cost leadership, this involves developing a range of products or services that is significantly better than the competitors.

Better in what sense? The important thing is that the customer should hold the differential element in sufficiently high regard—or, more specifically, a sufficient proportion of customers should do so—to ensure that the business achieves a significant market share, despite charging prices higher than its main competitors.

Focus Strategies

According to Porter, if a corporation does not possess sufficient attributes to dominate its market based on cost or to differentiate itself sufficiently, it must do whatever it takes to *avoid taking the middle way*.

In practice, the absence of any real strategy will condemn it to be supplanted in high-volume markets by those of its competitors that benefit from lower costs, while losing more demanding customers to corporations that have developed true differentiation.

In such circumstances, Porter therefore recommends a strategy of *focus*, which involves opting for a more tightly defined field of play as regards customers or products.

Indeed, it is easier for a corporation to develop a competitive advantage within a limited market segment where it will be able to either exercise cost leadership or to differentiate itself from competitors.

For that strategy to succeed, ideally you need your chosen market to be sufficiently small not to attract major competitors, while requiring sufficient dedicated investment to discourage other small competitors.

In the airline sector, Southwest Airlines deployed this strategy to become one of the most admired corporations in the world by focusing exclusively on domestic flights within the United States, using only secondary airports and a single type of aircraft.

Even giants focus. Coca-Cola has built a dominant position within a single market for alcohol-free beverages, without ever seeking to become a generalist food retailer, unlike its major competitors. Disney has built an empire without ever straying from the single sphere of family entertainment.

"Blue Ocean" Strategies

Is there an alternative to the three types of strategy described earlier?

It was in 2005 that two INSEAD business school lecturers, W. Chan Kim and Renée Mauborgne, opened a new page in strategic thinking with the brilliant concept of the "Blue Ocean strategy."

Upon completing a huge research project covering hundreds of corporations, these two researchers discovered that many outstanding success stories did not correspond to any of the three strategy types that Michael Porter had theorized about for 30 years.

For Porter, strategy is defined as the management of a war conducted against enemies within a specific market area.

Yet certain businesses, such as Cirque du Soleil, Swatch, and Nintendo (with its Wii console) have succeeded in avoiding face-to-face combat with its competitors by creating *new markets*. How did they achieve this?

A closer look at these cases reveals that in each instance the corporations *liberated themselves from the rules of the game for their industry.*

Firstly, they built highly competitive cost structures. Unlike their competitors, Cirque du Soleil does not use animals in its shows, Swatch does not use noble materials, and the Wii (Nintendo) offers only mediocre image definition. At first sight, one might therefore categorize their strategies among those based on "cost leadership."

However, they also included, significantly, elements from other business sectors in their respective products: Cirque du Soleil presents high-quality musical productions; Swatch was the first watchmaker to introduce fantasy into product design; and the Wii was the first gaming console based on motion detection.

These strategies therefore did not arise from a choice between cost leadership and differentiations, but incorporated both!

Furthermore, the key factor is that they do not seek to attack existing competitors, but to attract individuals or organizations *who are not yet anyone's customers* in their respective industries! Thus, the Wii took tens of millions of consumers (young girls, the elderly, etc.) who had never held a joystick in their lives and introduced them to video gaming.

The main consequence of these strategies, when they succeed, is the creation of new markets within which competition is completely nonexistent—sometimes for years on end.

Strategies and Combined Activities

Whichever of these great strategic models it selects, a business must protect itself against immediate imitation by competitors.

To do this, it is often essential to develop *a coherent and specific set of activities*, which is much more difficult to copy than a simple commercial product.

Thus, the IKEA model does not merely rely upon aesthetically pleasing, functional furniture but affordable mass-produced self-assembly furniture. It is based upon a complete model that includes, for example, easy-access parking, in-store child-care facilities, affordable on-site family catering, and the easy selection and shipment of products.

In the case of Apple, again it is the unique combination of activities such as physical products combined with the facility to order music online via iTunes and App Store apps shopping that enabled it to achieve the second highest stock market capitalization in the world in 2010, as well as the coveted title of the world's most admired company.

Strategies of Business Units, Businesses, and Conglomerates

Large organizations inevitably undertake multiple activities.

Each of these is often pursued in a specific context: products, customers, competitors, technologies, economic models, and key factors in success vary from one to another.

That is why, beyond a certain level of complexity, corporations are usually organized into business units. Whether or not it is a subsidiary, each of these institutions is responsible for the profitable development of its business within a boundary defined by its trade or market.

Some of those units are akin to one another in particular aspects of their business: use of the same technology, internal customers/supplier relationships, complementarity or even competition vis-à-vis a given category of customers. For example, this is generally the case with mass-marketed products.

In other cases, those units have no professional proximity to one another. What really is the common ground between Tesco's involvement in retailing and in financial services or between the Virgin Atlantic airline and the Virgin Media did cable TV? We therefore refer to *conglomerates* to describe highly diverse business groups that are essentially bound by financial ties.

These different situations can coexist at different levels within a single organization.

Thus, the Sky News and Sky Sports television channels coexist within the BSkyB group. Although it carries out various activities, BSkyB focuses on a single strand—information and entertainment—and can be viewed as a *business*.

At a higher level, BSkyB is itself partly (and potentially wholly) owned by News Corp., a conglomerate active in the media, publishing, entertainment, and the internet.

There are therefore three levels at which strategy is defined.

At the level of a *conglomerate* (e.g., Tesco), by necessity the strategy remains general in its formulation. Here financial issues and risk distribution are important: for example, certain activities may lend themselves to achieving growth, others liquidity, and some others stability.

At the level of a *business* (BSkyB), the strategy mainly seeks to use clear directives to maximize the synergy between its various institutions to the benefit of their shared economic and commercial ambitions.

At the level of the *business unit* (e.g., Sky Sports), the aim is to establish a sustainable competitive advantage within a very specific professional sphere.

The Strategic Initiative Concept

According to Michael Porter, "*Most executives think they have a strategy when they really don't, at least not a strategy that meets any kind of rigorous, economically grounded definition?*"

In contrast, all of them are capable of defining their *most important priorities*: winning over customers of a particular type, launching a major new product range, reorganizing production to improve efficiency, intensifying service innovation, etc.

That is why in this book we shall also use the word *strategy* to refer to a corporation's major competitive orientation and principal initiatives.

What Can Strategy Expect of Training?

Firstly, we need to understand how strategy needs training, before we define the key objectives that are to be assigned to it.

Implementing Strategy Relies Principally upon the Workforce!

As we said in the introduction, most strategies fail because they are badly implemented.

Training is therefore of great importance from several perspectives; it not only helps the corporation to carry out its chosen activities, but it also helps to secure the competitive advantage that it desires.

For a corporation to be able to implement its business strategy, the primary requirement is that it should *possess the skills needed to perform its activities effectively*.

Let us examine three examples of British and American businesses.

Once a British fixed-line telecommunications operator, BT has now become an integrated international operator with a strong commitment to the internet and associated services.

Once an American lighting business, General Electric now encompasses everything from media through infrastructure and high technology to finance.

Once a building society, Halifax is now a full-status bank before moving on as a merged concern to offer its customers the full range of international financial services from insurance to investment.

We can see that when strategy requires fundamental change, the role of training is to ensure that a sufficient number of employees are up to the job of producing the work expected.

This is the particular purpose of major induction programs for new staff and of occupational retraining.

The main challenges relate to the number of people involved, the need to limit the associated costs, and the need for effectiveness: the requirement is to enable a lot of people to carry out tasks that are new to them within very little time while deploying a reasonable volume of resources.

Beyond this initial fundamental imperative, training must allow the business to *secure its competitive advantage* within its strategic business unit(s).

Thus, cost-leadership strategies require you to achieve higher productivity and better performance levels than your competitors at each stage of the value chain, while using fewer resources and often a workforce that is predominantly underqualified.

Certain skills are crucial, such as *sourcing* and negotiating over purchases or managing business that has been extensively outsourced—including to subcontractors operating in low-cost countries. Likewise, at every level you need employees who are capable of handling large volumes efficiently, both as regards logistics and on an administrative level.

In the case of differentiation strategies, the challenge for the business is to ensure that the difference is actually perceived and valued by the market.

For this to be the case, that difference needs to be felt by all employees and not just those who are in contact with customers.

In his book *Change to Strange*, Daniel M. Cable[3] suggests that "a business can only differentiate itself by building a different, that is to say strange workforce" (page number).

The devil is in the detail: for example, you cannot consistently offer a customer top-of-the-range services if within the corporation there is negligence in the provision of services between internal suppliers and customers. Training must therefore *help all staff to adopt sufficient discipline,* in all their work, to ensure that the corporation maintains and increases its distinctiveness.

When a business opts for a focus-based strategy, once again training plays a key role.

To dominate a market segment consistently, a corporation must effectively develop a set of skills perfectly suited to that segment and of such a high standing that it is almost impossible for a competitor seeking rapid success to match them.

"Blue Ocean" strategies require personnel to know how to work outside the standards of their profession and to satisfy new customers who have different expectations.

Original business combinations require you to ensure that staff members doing jobs that do not usually have any connection cooperate effectively with one another.

Lastly, the deployment of strategic initiatives requires excellent execution at every level of the business.

It is true that training is not the only means of ensuring that tasks are completed to an excellent standard.

Indeed, within certain limits, a corporation can "buy in" skills by recruiting people who are already experts or by outsourcing certain activities. It can also "mechanize" activities and reduce its dependence on human intervention.

Businesses also possess the means of *reducing* training needs. For example, they can provide staff, at their work stations, with tools that allow them to have immediate access to the information required and giving them step-by-step guidance at the precise point when they carry out a task for the first time. This is the role played by the so-called EPSS (Employee Performance Support Systems) tools.

Nevertheless, however excellent it may look on paper, a strategy cannot succeed without effective training.

The question that then arises is: Exactly what types of objectives should training pursue to serve a strategy well?

Skills: Indispensable but Insufficient

The initial response that comes to mind is *skills* development.

Skills are generally considered quite different from knowledge in that they always combine *knowledge* with *expertise* and *interpersonal abilities*.

Skills are a kind of knowledge *obtained from the business*—which has become an "educational system"—and *validated through action*.

Indeed, the concept has the great merit of focusing training on the capacity of the individual to *implement* his or her newly acquired abilities. In practice, we usually define skills as the *capacity of an individual to resolve a given problem, in a given context*.

Viewed from a strategic perspective, developing skills is therefore an absolutely core objective of training.

This challenge is so important that the word now undergoes an infinite number of transformations: skills audit, skills standards, skills management or even skills-based management, skills planning, etc.

However, everyone could already see that for things to work, it was not enough for an individual to be "capable of resolving a given problem, in a given context."

In other words, improving *skills* is not enough to achieve *excellence*.

The fact that an individual is *capable* of resolving a problem does not allow you to anticipate that person's propensity for putting this into *practice*.

In our lives we are now surrounded by a multitude of problems (relating to our homes, our cars, our weight, or our family) that we would probably be *capable* of resolving but that we currently leave unaddressed, for all sorts of reasons. Capacity is insufficient; you also need *the desire to act*.

In addition, the fact that *on their own*, individuals may each be capable of resolving a given problem in a given context does not guarantee that *the organization* to which they belong will produce a better performance overall.

The history of sport is replete with cases of teams comprising players with exceptional skills that were unable to defeat lesser opponents.

If individuals do not share the same comprehension of words, situations, and priorities, individual skills will be insufficient to ensure collective excellence.

In short, the effective deployment of a strategy requires personnel not only with the appropriate *skills*, but also with a high level of individual *commitment* and a strong *common culture*.

Skills, commitment, and common culture: any policy, program, or training initiative devoted to a strategy should pursue objectives at these *three* levels.

This has considerable consequences for both the design and the deployment of training initiatives. We shall gradually discover this over the course of the coming chapters.

But are we not expecting too much of training? How effective is it really?

Training in the Dock

Let us delve back in time for a moment to the first decade of this millennium.

Small and big businesses alike were living in an environment transformed by extraordinarily rapid change.

Within a few years, the Internet and new communications technologies would revolutionize the economic models of entire sectors. Globalization was creating new competitors as well as new markets and was causing a massive shift in the world's centre of gravity toward Asia. Multiple mergers and acquisitions were leading to the emergence of new megacorporations that controlled most of the capital and investment and established new rules by which markets had to play.

Probably never in history had training needs been so huge.

In the emerging countries, within a few years they needed to prepare hundreds of millions of people to adopt the most modern methods of production, distribution, and even research and development.

In the developed countries, they needed to encourage all the new generations to position themselves in often highly skilled occupations that were less easy to "relocate." Yet they also needed to help people already in work to quickly adopt "best practices" as these alone would allow the organizations employing them to maintain their competitiveness and to survive.

Yet within businesses, training methods had still changed little since the postwar years.

It is true that training had made some progress. However, compared to the revolutions experienced in production, marketing, and customer service, thus far it had been quite slow to adapt.

For initial training, it was accepted that students had to listen to lecturers, carry out some practical work in groups, and then revise alone, before presenting themselves for examinations and competitions that principally allowed them to prove that they had duly memorized and interpreted the information provided.

For continuous training, more often than not a small group of 10 or so people was assembled with a trainer who shared his or her expertise while offering participants the opportunity to work on a few case studies.

E-learning had appeared, but its use generally remained marginal. More sophisticated tools, such as "serious games" inspired by video gaming were starting to be developed, but still without proving that they had a practical purpose to justify the cost involved. In truth, as we are now realizing, the first generation web—the so-called Web 1.0—was of limited benefit in terms of training.

Above all, though, training as a whole was finding it ever harder to convince people that it was effective.

In the business world, training was ever more frequently the subject of three criticisms.

First, the common criticism is that training *costs too much money and, more importantly, it took up too much time* in an environment where those two key resources were in short supply.

The sums devoted to training were indeed astronomical. In France, they amounted to almost €30bn per annum for continuous vocational training and sandwich courses alone, of which more than 40% was payable directly by businesses. Yet businesses controlled their costs as tightly as they could and no longer hesitated to question the value of training expenditure.

The time taken by training was also ever more difficult to reconcile with the imperatives of organizations operating on a just-in-time basis.

Secondly training is generally viewed to have failed to produce *a visible and indisputable impact upon the performance* of individuals, groups, and organizations after it was completed.

A major corporation often invested tens of millions of euros per year in its training programs, but what did that achieve? It was generally impossible not only to measure this but also to *identify* it, such was the general ineffectiveness of the training.

Lastly, and perhaps most worryingly, for those who believed in training, it largely benefited only *those who needed it least.*

Within a particular category of employees, training often accentuated inequality. Many training managers noticed this: only the most motivated, highest-performing individuals benefited from each training course. The others, those who were struggling to do their jobs, were generally the least satisfied: "*It was all theory*"; "*I already knew all that.*"

You might think, therefore, that training no longer has much use.

The Training Revolution Gets Underway

Let us return now to the years from 2010.

The most advanced major corporations are setting new objectives for training, which focus much more directly on strategy implementation and collective economic performance.

They are questioning the most widely accepted educational principles so as to drastically reduce the cost and time absorbed by training, while increasing its effectiveness.

They are using new technology and new tools—often connected to the meteoric rise of Web 2.0—and are bringing training into the everyday life of their company, their staff, their customers, and their partners, with the aim of ensuring that it finally benefits them all.

Over the recent months, the author, his partners, and their teams have had the opportunity to help Renault to plot the training of its 120,000 employees in the group's new values. L'Oréal has asked us to develop training packages designed for all its managers worldwide on subjects connected to personnel recruitment, evaluation, and development. Another large industrial group has invited us to train all its buyers in China, India, Japan, Brazil, the United States, and Europe. Each time this has involved methods that would have been unthinkable just a few years ago, as well as more ambitious objectives, shorter durations, and more effective systems.

Those corporations, among others, have understood that 2010–2020 is the era of the training revolution and, even more crucially, the era of *convergence between strategy and training.*

Key Points to Remember

- A business needs training not only to access the skills necessary to carry out its activities, but also and above all to *secure its competitive advantages through practical excellence* at every level of the business.
- Training is designed to develop skills, but it offers so much more.
  - The effective deployment of a strategy requires not only personnel with the appropriate skills, but also a high level of commitment and a strong common culture.
- People increasingly struggle to believe that training is effective.
  - In senior managers' eyes, it costs too much and takes too long.
  - It often fails to produce a visible and indisputable impact on performance.
  - It generally only benefits those who need it the least.
- A training revolution is underway.
  - Training is much more directly connected to strategy implementation and to the quest for excellence.
  - The teenies will be the era of convergence between strategy and training.

Recommendations

Training packages connected to the implementation of your strategy	Already achieved!	More or less ...	Not yet achieved
Are they designed and managed by people who have fully *understood the organization's strategic priorities?*			
Is their purpose to *ensure that a sufficient number of employees achieve the level required to produce the work expected?*			
Is their objective also to allow the business to secure specific *competitive advantages?*			

Are they systematically and specifically designed to simultaneously develop *skills, commitment, and a common culture?*			
Do they consume less time and fewer financial resources each year, while proving just as effective?			
Do they have an *indisputable impact on the performance* of people and of the organization?			
Do they specifically contribute to the progress made by *all* personnel, not just those who need it least?			
Do *senior managers* view them as a key lever for rolling out corporate strategy and achieving excellence?			
Do they rely upon *explicit, innovative educational principles* directed at the quest for effectiveness?			
Do they take full advantage of *2.0 technologies* and new tools to be integrated into the daily life of the business?			

CHAPTER 2

The Straight and Narrow Path to Excellence

Training Leads to Expertise, If and Only If …

In 1968, the Vietnam War was at its height. The United States had committed two of its great armed forces to the aerial combat. On average, the consistently excellent US Air Force shot down two enemy aircrafts for every one lost. The US Navy was finding life more difficult, seeing its success rate decline from an identical two-to-one ratio to a poor near parity within 2 years.

The US Navy had to respond. Near San Diego, California, it set up a revolutionary new training institution, the Navy Fighter Weapons School, also known as "Top Gun" and popularized by the film of the same name. Aerial combat was halted for a year, as training got under way.

When it resumed, the Air Force, which had not benefited from Top Gun training, started hitting its two-for-one ratio again. In contrast, the Navy achieved astonishing performance levels, on average shooting down 12 enemy aircraft for each one that it lost. It sustained this level until the end of the war.

That was just the start. Bolstered by the lessons learned from the Top Gun experiment, in 1980 the army set up the National Training Center (NTC) at Fort Irwin, California. Ten years later, it was recording the improved success in battle of units that had spent 4 weeks

(*Continued*)

(*Continued*)

at the NTC. Across hundreds of operations, it found that regiments or brigades had increased their success rate fivefold, combined arms teams were performing 15 times better, and light infantry sections had improved by a ratio of 30.

In the early 1990s, when the first Gulf War broke out, the US-led allied forces neutralized within a few days an Iraqi army which was thought to be very well equipped and trained. According to several US generals, the outcome would have been identical if the two armies had swapped their hardware. The crucial asset for the United States was the NTC.

Over the course of those decades marked by two horribly blood-soaked (and perhaps, let us be blunt, futile) wars, the US Army thereby very discreetly made a major discovery: well-designed and well-executed training is the most effective weapon of all.[1]

The implications of this are enormous. Firstly, consider finance. Training can produce better results, much more quickly, for a fraction of the cost of a major investment in a new generation of fighter planes or warships. Now think about the related intelligence and information. Military chiefs can no longer assess an enemy's power simply by observing their stock of hardware and equipment. Knowing how their opponents train and prepare their troops is a more useful way to predict their effectiveness in combat.

Lastly, pay attention to the strategic implications. If training can be so crucial in determining the success of a nation's military, it will probably also influence the success of the strategy adopted by a business, an authority, or an entire country.

Nevertheless, not all training programs have such spectacular effects. In many cases, the impact of such programs is marginal or even indiscernible. How can we explain that? What are the precise characteristics of training programs capable of generating spectacular and lasting success? How can we apply those characteristics to our work when developing the skills required to implement a business strategy?

Over the course of this chapter, you will discover …
- *… research findings on the development of expertise and excellence.
  Following in the footsteps of Professor Anders Ericsson, you will
  take a fresh look at talents as varied as Mozart and Tiger Woods,
  and assess the characteristics of work that leads to excellence.*
- *… the keys factors in effective strategy-oriented training …
  Having woken up to the fact that current training often contains
  all the seeds of its own failure, you will be relieved to identify
  principles that will allow you to radically increase its effectiveness*

Expertise Is Only Acquired Through a Certain Form of Systematic Coaching

It is 1976 and we are in Sweden.

A brilliant student, K. Anders Ericsson, has just received his
doctorate in psychology from the University of Stockholm. This shy but
pleasant young man with a passion for his work is as yet unaware that
he will unearth one of the most important discoveries in the history of
mankind.

Ericsson is to spend more than 30 years (he is still going) carrying out
in-depth research into one central issue: Exactly how do you become one
of the world's top experts in a particular discipline?

The End of the Natural Talent Myth

In sport, science, or the arts, the performance of certain individuals is
so much better than that of the casual practitioner that we often tend to
attribute this to an innate talent.

This belief is reinforced by the precocity of many great virtuosos,
champions, and experts.

How could Mozart have composed major works when he was barely
out of adolescence, other than possessing some divine gift? How could
Andre Agassi, Tiger Woods, or Bobby Fischer have taken the respective
worlds of tennis, golf, or chess by storm at such a young age if it were not
thanks to some *natural talent*?

The extraordinary ability that these individuals demonstrate lends weight to the thesis. For example, how can we explain the ability of a top chess player to play several matches simultaneously, while imagining hundreds of potential combinations of moves, sometimes without even looking at the board?

It is to these questions (and some others) that Anders Ericsson responds after dozens of years of research covering fields as diverse as golf, chess, football, music, surgery, and software design.

He is interested, for example, in violin playing.

He discovers that it is statistically impossible to predict which of a group of beginners will succeed in becoming top musicians by merely observing their first few steps in their chosen discipline.

Turning his attention to experienced violinists, he gets dozens of them to complete a very thorough questionnaire designed to identify the common points of the very best violinists.

The results brook no argument. At the age of eighteen, those deemed to be absolutely outstanding have accumulated an average of 7,500 hours practice with their instrument, whereas "very good" musicians have done no more than 5,300, and good amateurs about 3,400.

The most striking finding is that there seem to be no exceptions to the rule: for example, none of the members of the first group have practiced as little as those in the second group and none of the members of the second group have practiced as much as those in the first group.

All the other studies carried out by Ericsson, across a wide variety of disciplines, produced the same findings: it is the cumulative amount of work over the years that essentially determines the degree of excellence.

From this perspective, the case of Mozart becomes easier to understand.

Wolfgang's father, Leopold Mozart, was an established composer and musician with a particular passion for teaching music to children. His treatise on the fundamental principles of violin playing was to remain an authoritative work for decades.

A disciplinarian father, he imposed an intensive program of music lessons on his 3-year-old son. He subsequently stopped composing to devote himself full-time to Wolfgang's tuition.

His son's first compositions were not entirely his own work. In fact, Mozart's first four piano concertos, composed when he was 11 years old, contain no original music but combine the work of other composers. His next three works, composed when he was sixteen, were also arrangements based on the work of Johann Christian Bach, with whom he had studied in London. None of his works from this period are now considered to be great music. Indeed, they are rarely performed or recorded.

The first work of Mozart that can indubitably be called a masterpiece, its status confirmed by the number of different recordings that are available, is his Piano Concerto No. 9, composed when he was 21. Although still very young, by then Wolfgang had already absorbed 18 years of exceptionally intense coaching.

Contrary to popular belief, masterpieces never came fully formed from Mozart's fertile imagination. On the contrary, original manuscripts still existing reveal that Mozart was forever correcting, reworking, or rewriting whole passages or setting aside entire sections of scores for months or years.

Lastly, recent studies have enabled scholars to draw up a "precocity index" for pianists. Compared to an average of 100, Mozart rated 130, which is remarkable. Yet certain twentieth century prodigies, who have benefited from more modern learning and coaching methods rack up ratings of 300–500.

In chess, when Bobby Fischer became an international grandmaster at the age of fifteen, he had been practicing chess compulsively for about 10 years, having laid out chessboards in every room of his family home and having spent hours in the classroom imagining new combinations.

In his moving autobiography, Andre Agassi describes the crazy daily training schedule imposed on him by his father throughout his childhood. Other celebrities as different as Michael Jackson and Tiger Woods also reached the peak of their respective disciplines after a childhood almost entirely devoted to learning, and then polishing their skills.

Thus, the extraordinary abilities of the greatest experts and virtuosos are not innate.

If you need convincing, it is sufficient to note another observation made by Anders Ericsson during his research: the skills developed by people capable of very high degrees of excellence are very narrow and not readily transferable.

Those artists deemed to be the most creative therefore do not generally display that quality when they undergo tests in disciplines other than their speciality.

Likewise, years after a game, the top chess champions are capable of re-creating every move on the board. However, if they are given a memory test using words or playing cards, for the most part they do no better than low-level players.

Lastly, we can cite the instructive case of the Hungarian László Polgár, who was born in 1946. As a chess specialist, he wanted to convince the entire world that genius was a matter of learning. In order to demonstrate the merits of his thesis, one day he launched an appeal to find a wife who would agree to bear children for him and to help him to turn them into chess champions.

Klara, who was then a Hungarian teacher in the Ukraine, responded to that appeal. László and Klara devoted years to initiating their three daughters into chess and putting them through rigorous training.

The girls made exceptional progress and even became national heroines when they formed a team that beat the Soviets for the first time in history.

It is quite clear: "natural talent" is a myth. We now need to understand what type of training and coaching will allow us to develop excellence.

In Search of Deliberate Practice

Anders Ericsson was not content to update the myth of talent; he also deciphered the codes for acquiring expertise.[2]

In so doing, he discovered that practice alone is never enough to allow you to achieve a high degree of expertise.

It is true that running regularly increases your physical endurance and that lifting weights builds strength. Likewise, for someone who has suffered from a phobia, experiencing regular contact with the object of that phobia can enable them to gradually *build their confidence*.

Unfortunately, however, spending days on end playing golf will never turn you into a champion.

Indeed, although practicing an activity regularly allows you to acquire some ability and to improve your consistency, it is quite inadequate for achieving excellence: in reality, after a period of progress, your performance tends to stagnate. Subsequent progress is more marginal and very unpredictable.

Only *systematic, focused* coaching allows you to achieve a high level of performance. Such coaching, which Ericsson describes as *deliberate practice*, is defined by the following characteristics.

Firstly, it is work carried out strictly with the *goal of improvement*. The mere fact of performing a task as part of your job or leisure activity cannot therefore constitute *deliberate practice*.

Secondly, this self-improvement work is organized according to *precise and limited objectives*: it involves improving one particular aspect of your performance at a time, such as a crosscourt topspin backhand for a tennis player.

It is carried out in a *highly repetitive manner* and is the subject of *precise and regular feedback*.

The effectiveness of this method is staggering, firstly when acquiring the skills to complete elementary tasks and then for ever more demanding assignments.

Thus, Ericsson's first experiment, 30 years ago, consisted in training an individual to hear and then repeat a random series of numbers. After about 20 hours of coaching, the sequence of numbers had increased from seven to twenty. After 200 hours of coaching, the subject was capable of remembering series of more than 80 numbers.

When tackling complex real-life situations, experiments carried out with US Army fighter pilots demonstrate that you need to go through various stages.

Initially, coaching involves achieving excellence in *each basic task*.

Once the pilot has fully mastered these, he must train himself to *connect the different tasks* in a simplified environment.

It is only then that the pilot is confronted with *major adversity*, applying the tactics and techniques habitually employed by the enemy.

Lastly, the final training phase places the pilot under multiple constraints: sleep deprivation, equipment breakdowns, and unpredictable adversaries.

However, the coaching of people who have achieved very high performance levels is principally determined by the volume and regularity of the work done over the years.

Indeed, whatever the discipline observed, Ericsson noted that the achievement of a very high performance level required roughly the same amount of work: 2 to 3 hours per day, every day of the week (including weekends) for a period of 10 to 30 years.

For sports person, the cumulative duration of *deliberate practice* is generally no less than 10 years. For top scientists, it is closer to 30 years.

Thus, whatever their discipline, Ericsson claims that you need at least 10,000 to 15,000 hours of systematic, focused coaching to become an expert.

Such a set of revelations is of the utmost importance.

It shows that, in practice, focused training and coaching can change an individual's destiny.

It provides powerful arguments for those who believe in human beings and the individual potential for development. Human beings are plastic and flexible. They can work on their own expertise as on a noble material and can progress without limits.

It also confirms that training constitutes a crucial sphere of activity for companies and for any human organization.

Most significantly, however, when applied to the issue of strategy implementation, it proves that employees can master any new professional task, provided that they devote a sufficient quantity and quality of training to it.

Unlearning and Maintaining Excellence

Various research carried out by the US Army has facilitated a better understanding of the conditions required to maintain expertise in a particular series of tasks.

Unlearning is a normal and inevitable phenomenon. After a training course, participants tend to forget a proportion of the content, which affects their performance. Naturally, the rate of unlearning is much higher if the participants do not put their training into practice.

Thus, in 1998, at the start of every *3-week* training course, on average the Navy squadrons met 30% of their targets.

At the end of each course, the success rate very consistently reached 70%. Unfortunately, after *3 months* without regular practical implementation, that rate fell back just as consistently to 40%.

To be more specific, it seems that skills requiring memory and thought crumble more rapidly than those requiring physical and manual abilities.

While *overlearning*, which consists in learning the same thing several times over, is of little use over the course of a single training session, it proves very effective at rapidly taking skills temporarily "lost" through unlearning and restoring them to their proper level.

Thus, 3 months after a 3-week training course, a *3-day* refresher course is sufficient to ensure that the shooting success rate of Navy squadrons returns to 70%.

In the case of pilots, the pace of "unlearning" after training is just as consistent.

This means that if a pilot does not fly for six to twelve months, his/her skills fall below an acceptable level. Light usage makes scarcely any difference: pilots who fly for 1 hour per month lose their ability at a rate comparable (to within 10%) to those who do not fly at all.

All this erosion of skills takes place within the first year: the training time required to get a pilot back up to standard is identical whether that pilot has not flown for 1 year or 3.

These experiments highlight several key principles.

Firstly, training must be administered *just before it is put into practice*. In the case of pilots, for example, any training completed more than 6 months before flying has almost no operational effectiveness.

This means that ideally training must be *divided into a series of short sessions* to allow the elementary skills acquired to be put into practice each time and to limit the scale of the unlearning.

Lastly, the training must give rise to *short but regular refresher sessions*, in order to effectively refresh skills and performance levels, which involves a minor investment compared to the initial training burden.

Deliberate Practice Within
a Business Is Possible

Given the importance of Anders Ericsson's discoveries, we must ask about their application to the strategic training carried out by businesses.

Do the training packages that we are familiar with allow employees to benefit from the powerful effectiveness of *deliberate practice*?

If that is not yet the case, how can we transpose the characteristics highlighted by Ericsson, which often involve a whole lifetime's work, to training programs at best limited to a few days?

Traditional Training Programs and Deliberate Practice

Let us imagine the case of a business whose strategy requires a series of new product launches and new organizations.

One of the essential skills to be developed is the ability of teams to manage projects.

The business therefore commits itself to a series of training programs intended for all middle managers.

Let us follow a particular employee—we will call her Vanessa—who is taking part in a project management training course.

Before she attends the seminar, scheduled to last two days, she is asked to read a few reference articles on the subject and to complete a preparatory document in which she describes the detailed characteristics of the projects for which she is responsible.

Once she is in the room, Vanessa takes part in an introductory discussion during which everyone is able to get to know one another. To liven up the exercise and to establish a group dynamic, the trainer asks each participant to present a neighbor, having allowed the group a few minutes to prepare for this initial exercise.

As the presentations are often vague and sometimes include major errors, those involved generally have to clarify or correct the accounts of their respective career histories and the specification of their current responsibilities.

The trainer takes advantage of this to make the group aware of the importance of listening. An animated debate then ensues on this subject. Vanessa raises the matter of the difficulties she faces in getting a hearing within a corporation whose hierarchical structures often override project-based structures.

Finally, having presented an overview of the seminar, the trainer launches into the first session, addressing the general preparation for a project.

Rather than giving a theoretical talk, he presents the group with a fascinating case study.

Divided into small working groups, the course members get to grips with a complex case study in which they have to analyze a large number of parameters in order to develop a project road map.

The various subgroups take turns to present their conclusions. The trainer asks them questions and allows other participants to have their say. Many observations are made, often of great significance. Fascinated, Vanessa takes reams of notes. The trainer concludes by summing up each team's apparent strong points and those few errors to avoid next time, with some simple and specific recommendations for improvement.

The seminar then alternates between brilliant presentations by the trainer, fruitful plenary debates, and very encouraging work in subgroups.

These activities are sometimes interspersed with role plays during which two participants conduct an interview in front of the rest of the group. At the end of the role play, each person is given personal advice about the strengths that they could exploit and the weaknesses that they could correct or control. Thus, Vanessa learns that she can be confident of her organizational sense and her natural authority, but that she needs to take the time to listen more to the concerns of her customers and partners in order to better involve them in her projects.

Vanessa was delighted with her seminar. When she came to complete her evaluation form, she gave it top marks and recommended that all her colleagues, in turn, should attend the same course.

The human resources manager was all smiles when she read through the evaluation summary that the training manager had sent her. She was absolutely convinced that they had selected the correct topic, contents, and training agency.

The problem was that *in no way* did this training course corresponds to the principles identified by Ericsson as being characteristic of *deliberate practice*, whereas we know that these are essential to the development of excellence.

Indeed, like most corporate training courses that we are aware of, this one assigned very little time to *practical exercises*.

In practice, most time was devoted to listening to the trainer, debating with other participants, or even observing exercises carried out by other nonexperts: while all are useful methods, in reality, they are limited in effectiveness: "*imagine learning to swim without getting in the water.*"

Furthermore, when they are available, the exercises are generally *complex*, encompassing a number of wide-ranging educational objectives. In contrast, *deliberate practice* involves, at least initially, focusing on a limited number of very specific objectives.

While *deliberate practice* assumes that the practice is carried out with a *strict goal of improvement*, such complexity encourages the learner to devote their preparations to mastering not the skill that is to be developed, but the actual substance of the exercise.

It also renders *feedback* less effective. It is difficult to provide and to soak up given the number and variety of comments made during the exercise. In addition, it is even more difficult to apply as it generally covers too wide a range of concepts and skills.

More significantly, the exercises are almost never *repeated*, whereas a high degree of repetition is absolutely essential if progress is to be achieved. When the exercises are repeated, this often involves a change in roles, which makes self-improvement impossible.

Lastly, the training does not allow for the deployment of a series of different *phases of deliberate practice*: completely mastering elementary tasks, combining and connecting those tasks in a simplified environment, being immersed in a more realistic environment, and then undergoing training faced with a variety of extreme constraints.

Overall, Vanessa and her colleagues certainly learned some useful lessons from their seminar.

However, on completing the course there was little chance that they would notice tangible progress—and no doubt that the training had little impact upon the effective implementation of company strategy.

Does that mean that the principles discovered by Anders Ericsson cannot be applied to company training programs?

Dare We Challenge the Training Paradigms?

As we have seen, there is a great disparity between the principles developed by Ericsson and the characteristics of most training programs currently provided within corporations.

That disparity is unacceptable when training is a lever for the implementation of strategy.

We therefore need to do things differently now and to have the courage to challenge certain paradigms that underpin the design of training courses.

For example, it is generally accepted that you learn through *listening to the teacher*, through *discussions with your peers*, and through the *observation of others*.

It is also said that exercises serve to *raise awareness of your errors*, and that it is *experience* and *practice on the ground* that allow you to polish your skills.

All this is partially true, but with significant limitations.

Listening to the teacher is certainly one method of learning. However, most individuals find it very difficult to spontaneously *transpose* a theoretical concept to practical implementation. Likewise, in practice transposing lessons learned from one specific example to another example in a different context is very difficult for many people.

These abilities to transpose are actually connected to a special form of intelligence and education. This quality is overrepresented among senior managers and training designers, which partly explains the disparity that is often found between the quality of the concepts and examples presented during training and their poor use by trainees.

Similarly, discussions with peers and the observation of others offer only very debatable benefits.

It is true that "instructive modeling" has proven to be effective. Yet this requires the selection as examples of people with a perfect mastery of the tasks involved, and not employees with average performance levels or an inability to clearly distinguish between good and bad practice.

People can learn from errors, but by its very nature this process is slow and relatively unproductive. Indeed, research shows that people avoid committing themselves to actions likely to generate a feeling of disquiet or expose a lack of self-esteem. Furthermore, if those errors occur during the real activity, such learning can prove costly.

As for experience and practice, Ericsson has demonstrated their limits.

It is therefore essential to also accept that excellence principally stems from *focused and systematic coaching*, which is clearly distinct from mere professional *practice* as it is carried out with the strict goal of improvement.

This requires several major changes compared to traditional methods.

In effect, each individual must be encouraged to train *individually* in each of the key skills that are to be acquired.

Each of the tasks required clearly revolves around a *limited* educational objective that is well understood. It is not designed to reveal "strong points" and "areas for improvement," but to lead to a complete mastery of the skill in question.

The precision of *feedback* is crucial, because it must allow trainees to set themselves one or two specific targets for progress and to immediately improve their performance.

It is absolutely essential that each individual should be able to *repeat* the same exercise several times until they have mastered it.

This is their only means of achieving sufficient mastery of the task to feel completely confident and to then reproduce the same performance when the real activity is undertaken after training.

Lastly, once the elementary skills have been acquired, the trainee learns to combine and to connect them in ever more difficult environments, always with a precise evaluation and with new targets for progress being set.

Although they are very different from traditional training methods, these principles are perfectly applicable to the business world.

Let us take the example of the repetition of exercises.

In January 2007, Adecco was seeking to add value to all its services. It was essential for its sales reps to provide clear, relevant, and convincing answers to customers' questions. So the company organized several seminars, each of which brought together about a hundred sales managers.

Half of the time was devoted to practical coaching. Organized in pairs, the participants simultaneously trained themselves to spend 2 minutes answering questions frequently asked by customers. After each round, the participant being trained received three specific recommendations for improvement from their partner. A series of several rounds was organized to allow them to achieve a good understanding of the issue. The roles were then reversed and various scenarios were explored.

At subsequent seminars, those managers got their branch managers to take part in the same exercises.

According to Jacques Delsaut, the Sales and Marketing Manager, *"that training was one of the main reasons for the exceptional growth in Adecco's operating profits in 2007."*[3]

Let us now address the potential for combining and connecting different elementary skills once these have been acquired.

An American Professor Steven Spear reports that when he was preparing his doctoral thesis on car production systems, he had the opportunity to work successively at Chrysler and Toyota installing the front passenger seat.

At Chrysler, the foreman responsible for training him explained: "Steve, the cars arrive on this line every 28 seconds, so that is how long you have to install the seat. I'll show you how to do it: first, you take this bit like this. Then you do this, then that, and then you put this right opposite that, then you tighten this and next you turn that."

This all seemed quite simple but when the first car came along Spear was unable to complete the operation properly. The foreman stopped the line and again showed him how to do it. When subsequent cars arrived, Spear again encountered problems and the line had to be stopped several more times: after an hour just four seats had been properly installed.

At Toyota, his experience was quite different. The foreman explained to Steve Spear: "Here are the seven stages required to install the front passenger seat. You'll only be allowed to learn stage two when you've demonstrated that you have fully mastered stage one. That might take a minute or an hour, or it might take until tomorrow, but it makes no sense to learn subsequent stages if you haven't mastered the initial stages."

Once he had fully mastered all the operations and was able to string them together, Spear took his place on the assembly line and systematically succeeded in installing all the seats within the time allocated.

At Chrysler, the training time was fixed, but the training outcome was variable and unpredictable.

At Toyota, the training time was variable, as it adapted to the trainee's pace of learning. However, the outcome was perfectly consistent and reliable.

In a quite different vein, diversity is at the heart of L'Oréal's values and strategy. Ensuring employment diversity requires managers to be professional in the way they conduct recruitment interviews. In particular, when evaluating candidates this requires that the biases inherent to any human assessment should be reduced to a minimum.

The "Manager Recruiting Talent" training course is offered to the group's managers worldwide. Given that they all have packed diaries, it lasts for just 1 day.

At first sight, when the subject is so complex it would seem difficult to cover every stage of *deliberate practice* in so little time.

Yet a solution has been found: once they have mastered each recruitment phase, the participants are put in pairs and *take turns*, assembling a full interview between them.

As it is impossible, in practice, to successively conduct and analyze two complete recruitment interviews at the end of a course—so that each person is completely trained in the recruitment process—the participants swap roles during the various phases of the interview. They can thereby learn to put together a full interview by alternately spending time in the shoes of the recruiter and of the candidate.

The Management Development Director, David Arnera, explains:

"It was important for our managers to acquire a policy, a stance, but also certain instincts. We needed to offer some meaning, but also a real opportunity to undertake a brief period of practical coaching. The benefits gleaned on every continent from that training demonstrate that we achieved that."

These various changes in training design require the capacity to properly define the key training objectives.

Indeed, it is common for corporations to *overestimate the amount of information that employees need* in order to apply a strategy in their everyday work. Too often, training is therefore overburdened with content, involving slides packed with text or training documents that weigh down briefcases on the day of a seminar but are never opened again.

In parallel, it is just as common for company trainers to *underestimate the training practice required* in order to acquire new instincts.

As we shall see in the next chapter, we must not reduce the purpose of training to the mere acquisition of instincts. However, strategy implementation does require such learning. Defining very precise teaching objectives is therefore crucial.

A Business Run According to Deliberate Practice

It is clearly essential that training initiatives should be characterized by *deliberate practice* if we want them to contribute effectively to strategy implementation.

As Anders Ericsson has demonstrated, it is still true that a few days training is insufficient: you need at least 10,000 hours to achieve excellence.

Furthermore, the mere accumulation of years of professional experience does not in itself provide the constant improvement necessary to the perfect execution of the tasks that contribute to the strategy.

However, three factors among others can help to ensure that daily activity is a source of constant progress for individuals.

The first factor is the promotion of a *feedback culture*.

Thus, the US Army was able to judge that the quality of "after action reviews" (AARs) was crucial in raising the individual and collective skills of its troops.

Significant work was done in the United States to ensure that senior grades learned to accept and listen to feedback from their personnel. It has been established that, among fighter pilots in Kuwait, those who had been trained by the US Air Force benefited much more from AARs than those who had been trained by most European armies.

Within corporations, this feedback culture is mainly seen in organizations that try to develop a *coaching approach* on the part of their managers.

This approach starts with observing each employee on a daily basis as they complete their tasks. Systematic observation of your employees going about their work is the only way to provide meaningful feedback: "ticking boxes is not enough."

With the employee, the manager–coach duly assesses the skills acquired and selects a few targets for progress. They help the employee to identify opportunities to put this into practice by deliberately entrusting particular tasks to them *with the aim of achieving an improvement*. Lastly, they assess progress and recognize effort.

The second way of introducing *deliberate practice* into a corporation is to encourage personnel to ritualize the *formal self-assessment* of their work.

Thus, a multinational that specializes in selling business services recently introduced a systematic process of this type.

Each sales representative has to formalize preparations for each set of negotiations by specifying their objectives, the key points of their strategy, and the specific skill that they mainly plan to rely on.

At the end of each visit, they note the results achieved, but above all the lessons learned from how the negotiations developed. They set personal objectives for progress in the next negotiations.

Each negotiating report is discussed with the sales manager during a monthly review.

The progress made is consistent and absolutely spectacular.

Lastly, the corporation can develop a *pilot* culture.

When each project is the subject of a series of pilot exercises designed to provide usable feedback, it becomes possible for pilot teams to be set precise targets for progress.

The monitoring of this progress in turn allows other staff members to be given role models to set benchmarks for them.

In conclusion to this chapter, the concept of *deliberate practice* is absolutely essential to the effective implementation of a strategy.

In many cases, training needs to be reinvented in order to give employees the opportunity to try and acquire specific skills, to train repeatedly, to benefit from precise feedback, and to perfect their mastery of elementary tasks before learning to combine and connect them in ever more difficult environments.

Looking beyond formal training, it is partly everyday work that must provide the opportunity for such coaching, thanks to manager–coaches, formal self-assessment rituals, and the development of a pilot culture.

This offers great untapped sources of progress and effectiveness, contributing to the practical implementation of a business strategy.

Naturally, there is then the issue of the *object* of the training: What needs should the training meet?

Some believe that the priority must be to eliminate or reduce *organizational* weaknesses.

Others think that above all training must be personalized and that skills standards must be used to overcome the shortcomings of each *individual*.

The next chapter, entitled *The Fascinating Mechanics of Progress*, wrong-foots each of these two approaches.

Key Points to Remember

- Whatever the discipline, expertise, and excellence result from *systematic and focused* training work called *deliberate practice* that is characterized by the following.
  - A strict goal of improvement.
  - Organization according to precise and limited objectives.
  - A high degree of repetition.
  - Regular precise feedback.
- This training successively addresses the following.
  - The acquisition of excellence in each basic task.
  - Then the connection of the different tasks in a simplified environment.
  - Then implementation in a realistic situation.
  - Lastly implementation under severe constraints.
- Performance maintenance requires that training should be administered *just prior to implementation*; it should be divided *into a series of short sessions*, and should be followed by *short but regular refresher sessions*.
- The vast majority of training carried out within corporations does not correspond *in any way* to the principles of *deliberate practice*.
- We therefore now need to do things differently.
  - Each individual must be encouraged to receive *individual training* in each of the key skills that they need to acquire.

- ○ Each of the tasks required is to clearly focus upon a *limited* educational objective. It is designed to achieve perfect mastery of the skill in question.
- ○ *Feedback* must allow the trainee to immediately improve his/her performance.
- ○ It is essential that each individual should have the opportunity to *repeat* the same exercise several times.
- ○ Once elementary skills have been acquired, the trainee learns to combine and connect these in even more difficult environments.
- • Looking beyond training, three elements can help to make everyday work a source of continuous progress for individuals.
  - ○ Promoting a *feedback culture* and developing a *coaching approach* among managers.
  - ○ Encouraging personnel to carry out the ritualized *formal self-assessment* of their work.
  - ○ Developing a culture of *pilot experiments* incorporating precise and systematic feedback.

Recommendations

The training connected to the implementation of our strategy ...	Yes!	More or less ...	Not yet
... Does it give a dominant role (at least 65%) to practical exercises?			
... Is it built around short sequences targeted upon very precise objectives for the acquisition of skills?			
... Does it allow each employee to train *individually*?			
... Does it allow each employee to train individually *in each subject*?			
... Does it allow each employee to train *several times* in each subject *until they acquire the skill in question*?			
... Does it provide each employee with very precise *feedback* focusing upon skills learning objectives?			
... Does it *successively* address the mastery of elementary tasks, the connection of those tasks, their application in a realistic situation, and then in extreme situations?			

… Is it administered *just prior to implementation?*			
… Is it *divided into a series of short sessions?*			
… Do they include *short but regular refresher sessions?*			
Is it promoted and complemented, on an everyday basis, thanks to a *strong culture of peer feedback?*			
Is it promoted and complemented on an everyday basis, thanks to *the widespread adoption of a coaching approach by line management?*			
Is it promoted and complemented on an everyday basis through *the widespread application of formal self-assessment rituals within the corporation?*			
Is it promoted and complemented on an everyday basis, thanks to the organization of pilot experiments, giving rise to precise and systematic feedback?			

CHAPTER 3

The Fascinating Mechanics of Progress

Different Challenges Require Different Training Responses

When Jean-Marie Descarpentries took charge of the Carnaud Group in the early 1980s, the French market leader in metal packaging was in a pitiful state. Turnover was stagnant, operating profits were wafer-thin, and it was making a net loss due to its hefty debt burden and high financial costs.

The corporation, which had a turnover of approximately £400m, had a stock market valuation of just £8m. The former flagship of the CGIP business empire, built around the forges of Nantes and developed among the canning plants of Concarneau, Brittany, was failing. Its ultimate fate seemed to hover between asset stripping, a lingering death, and brutal liquidation.

Descarpentries was an unusual CEO. As a graduate of a top French engineering school, consultant at McKinsey, paratroop officer, and trade union official, he was a bold choice to head up a failing conglomerate. However, endowed with a great capacity for listening, brilliant intelligence, inexhaustible energy, and an enthusiasm for communicating, he was the archetype of a charismatic leader. His knowledge and experience within the packaging industry had led to prominent roles in Saint-Gobain, where he had successfully turned round several struggling businesses. Over a private lunch, the representative of the principal shareholder, Ernest-Antoine Seillières, was quick to entrust

(*Continued*)

him with the keys to the boardroom. His brief was to do whatever was necessary to rescue the company.

Descarpentries was to turn Carnaud round and take it forward at a blistering pace. Over a 10-year period, turnover increased by an average of 29% per annum, while its share price rose 55 fold. During this great adventure, he also developed, almost by chance, a very simple and exceptionally useful system for interpreting the mechanisms for progress within an organization: *leadership dynamics*. It is this system that will guide us throughout this chapter.

To help determine his strategic priorities, Descarpentries brought together a new group of twenty people every 3 months to take a fresh look at the business. This group generally included newly appointed middle managers, plus executives who had just moved to a different role or department. On meeting each group, Descarpentries would ask the members to identify Carnaud's strengths and weaknesses, as they saw them, and then to select the major strength to maintain and the main weakness to eliminate. Over subsequent days, the board would systematically debate those issues and draw up action plans based on them.

After 3 years marked by strong growth in the group's results, Descarpentries produced a full summary of this operation to check whether the weaknesses had been eliminated and the strengths maintained. The findings of this summary report surprised and intrigued him. It turned out that although the situation of the business was improving, the groups were pointing out more and more weaknesses. In fact, *new weaknesses were appearing* at every meeting. For example, inadequate *benchmarking*[1] was cited as a weakness in Year Two, whereas nobody had mentioned it a year earlier.

Clearly, Carnaud had been no better at benchmarking in Year One. But the business had still been *unaware* of the issue. Only after the publication of a few press articles, some local experiments and the appearance of a few teething problems in Year Two, did people *think* to even cite benchmarking among the group's weaknesses. Thus, *the appearance of a weakness itself constituted progress.*

(*Continued*)

In addition, several other issues cited as weaknesses in Year One had not disappeared in Year Two but were now *cited as strengths*. For example, *the autonomy granted to business units* was seen as a weakness in Year One; some participants perceived it to be inadequate and poorly understood by head office, while others felt that it led to disparities in group strategy. In Year Two, after head office and business units had worked together to clarify policies, the autonomy granted to the latter was universally deemed to be a strength. Likewise, in Year Three, *benchmarking*, which had materialized as a weakness in Year Two, also became a strength.

There were often animated discussions as to whether a business activity was a strength or a weakness. The answer lay in comparing Carnaud's performance in a particular area with that of its direct competitors. If the group was not doing as well as its rivals, then the issue in question was a weakness. When it succeeded in outdoing them, that activity could be considered a strength. Thus, you never *eliminate* a weakness, but you can *convert it into a strength*, provided that you catch up with your competitors and then overtake them in the relevant area. Among other things, this means that you can only realistically address a small number of weaknesses at any one time.

There then remained the issue of whether the group's strengths were being maintained. Once more, an astonishing finding: *strengths were disappearing*. For example, *the autonomy granted to business units*, which had gone from being a weakness in Year One to a strength in Year Two, was no longer cited at all in Year Three. Likewise, *technical innovation*, which had been a strength in Year One, was no longer mentioned in either Year Two or Year Three. What had happened was that these factors had been fully assimilated by the organization and group members *no longer even thought to mention them*. They now formed part of the business *culture*.

So what becomes of such factors when they are incorporated into a company's organizational culture? They may be neglected and underused, providing no strategic benefits. Alternatively, they may be "refreshed" and become the subject of ambitious and vigorous action

(*Continued*)

(*Continued*)

plans. When this happens, they offer the business its most reliable competitive advantage, as they represent the factor that competitors find hardest to imitate.

Jean-Marie Descarpentries modeled an organization's leadership dynamics in the form of a very simple table:

Unknown	Weaknesses	Strengths	Culture

An organization progresses by shifting factors from the left to the right of the table above.

You need to continually introduce new, as yet *unknown* work issues and then experiment with those new issues, thereby creating new *weaknesses*. Next, you need to catch up and overtake your direct competitors in those areas in order to endow yourself with new *strengths*. The next step is to systematize and assimilate those strengths in order to enrich your *organizational culture* and then, finally, you have to use that culture to build and reinforce your business's position of *leadership* in its markets.

This interpretation of progress within organizations enables us to understand why merely tackling an organization's weaknesses cannot take the place of strategy. It is through its strengths, and particularly its culture, that a business builds its future leadership, and it is through innovation (currently *unknown* factors) that it prepares to lead the way over distant horizons. Such leadership dynamics apply just as much to *individuals* as they do to organizations. When someone discovers a task or activity with which they are unfamiliar, they gradually acquire the ability to perform it and then, in certain cases, develop such a ready expertise in that skill that it becomes second nature to them.

In this chapter, you will discover …

… that training must become "situational":

To sustain the implementation of a strategy, it is essential to examine the nature of the progress the organization expects to make. Training objectives and methods will have to vary widely, depending, for example, on whether you are introducing a new practice or making better use of an asset that is already deeply rooted in the business culture.

… that training can even be adapted to the situation of each individual …

In practice, a person who has to remedy a weakness must overcome problems very differently from those faced by someone who has to reinforce a strength.

Training in Support of Organizational Progress

Schematically, we can distinguish between four types of strategic challenges, depending on whether they involve introducing new activities, remedying weaknesses vis-à-vis the competition, further reinforcing strengths or capitalizing on the business culture.

Each type of challenge comes with its own particular training problems: we therefore need to imagine a *situational training exercise.*

Introducing New Practices into an Organization

For years temporary employment agencies have specialized in the provision of interim personnel. In many countries, their business is strictly defined by a whole raft of regulations.

When, In a major European country, when the government changed the regulation in 2005, the recruitment market suddenly opened up to temporary employment agencies.

Most of the players in the sector immediately opted to make the development of such services a strategic priority for growth.

Their task therefore was to set up an activity that was as yet unfamiliar to their teams.

They knew that they would require a learning period during which that new activity would not match the performance standards achieved by recruitment specialists. An *unknown* activity has to start by becoming a *weakness* before sufficient excellence is acquired for it to be converted into a *strength.*

How, under such circumstances, should you train your teams and enable them to implement the new strategy?

Experience leads us to make a number of recommendations.

It is essential to identify *pioneers* within the corporation.

Within any organization, most people can only start pursuing a new objective if the various *stages* allowing this to be achieved are explained to them specifically and precisely.

Others, a minority, like to think for themselves about the various options which enable them to achieve the expected outcome. Curious, audacious, and tenacious in response to setbacks, they enjoy experimenting, innovating, and blazing a trail.

Such people are the pioneers who must be given the responsibility for pilot operations, and the lessons they learnt will assist in the wider implementation of the strategic initiative.

Thus, it is essential to *build in-house models of success* before carrying out training on a wider basis.

In fact, programs relying exclusively on methods and practices brought in from outside are generally doomed to fail, because they do not suit the particular characteristics of that corporation, owing to scepticism among personnel or due to a combination of both these reasons.

It is therefore essential that the pilot should lead to the agreement of models that are simultaneously simple, precise, and specific.

As a first step, a few branches chosen from leading temporary employment agencies were given, as a pilot project, the initial responsibility for experimenting with the new economic model.

Secondly, the objectives sought must be *gradual*, in order to build confidence in teams through a series of "minor victories."

In practice, you cannot move an activity straight from the "unknown" column to the "strengths" column. You need to proceed in stages.

Lastly, for this new activity it is particularly important that *training should go hand in hand with implementation*: for staff, training must coincide with the commencement of practical application.

By its very nature, carrying out a new activity is stressful.

If you were to commence the activity without training, there is a risk that employees would embark on a downward spiral of failure.

If there is too long a gap between training and implementation, employees will feel insecure. "Avoidance" mechanisms will be put in place and the activity will not take off.

If implementation takes place without support (guidance, feedback, and monitoring), initial enthusiasm gives way to resignation in the face of setbacks.

Correcting a Business Weakness

There are many strategic projects that rely on existing skills and activities but that also require profound changes, especially to match leading competitors in a particular field.

Thus, in 2009 the management team of a large media company deemed it necessary to take better advantage of the synergies between its various teams.

It was true that project work had begun to expand several years previously, and there had already been remarkable progress in this area, such as in youth programming and major sports events.

However, until then there had been a distinct compartmentalization between the group's various channels and regional broadcasters, which still sometimes generated excessive use of resources when covering an event or producing a program.

To senior management eyes, it therefore became essential to develop the ability of teams to work "horizontally" outside hierarchical structures.

A strategically important training project was therefore rolled out, in tandem with structural changes: organization, process, equipment, etc.

Tackling a *collective weakness* is never easy. Almost inevitably, such initiatives arouse some resistance to change: the initial instinct of a corporate body is to defend the *status quo*.

In practice, this resistance stems from the organization's *habits*, comprising priorities, ways of acting, and ways of thinking inherited from the past. When strategy takes on habits, the latter almost always win.

The first objective of training, in such a situation, is not therefore to help people acquire new skills: the key element is that it should also help to change the habits of the organization.

In many cases, resistance to change arises because the corporate body is unaware of the scale of the *problem* (or *opportunity*) that gave rise to the strategic initiative that it is to implement.

Training must therefore bring about a *greater awareness of the importance and urgency of action.*

One means of achieving this is to put employees in a position where they will discover what is at stake, by looking at data, carrying out exercises, or being exposed to external evidence by customers, partners, or consultants.

In other situations, employees may not believe in the *solution*: maybe because the problem is seen as insoluble (i.e., fatalism), because they are unconvinced by the chosen remedies (i.e., scepticism) or even because the problem is not their responsibility and thus they are not responsible for resolving it.

In such circumstances, training must *"prove that it works."*

The best way of achieving this is often to rely on "positive deviants": these are employees who have already been successfully implementing, over a period of time, the practices that the business now wants to introduce across the board. It is much easier to accept the experience of your peers than solutions brought in from outside.

For example, at a large mobile telecom operator in Europe,[1] between 2003 and 2006, a strategic project sought to help managers to further increase staff commitment. Over 4 years, the number of employees who considered themselves "happy in (their) professional life" with their jobs, as measured by IPSOS, grew by 46%. One of the keys to the success of that operation was the sharing of best practice of the teams that had made the most progress over the previous 2 years. The operator's 1,500 managers were quick to pick up the gauntlet, and numerous initiatives were generated which ultimately resulted in reassuring data from employee satisfaction surveys.

There are yet other cases where resistance is connected to the fact that the change is perceived as a *threat*, either to employees' *interests* (their jobs, career prospects, working conditions, or job satisfaction) or to *values* to which they are attached.

Training must therefore offer *reassurance*, and often *clear goals.*

It can do this in various ways: by showcasing the favorable experiences of employees from pilot groups, by offering an experience of the positive new aspects of the job, or by linking future practices with familiar elements from the past and with long-cherished values.

In each case, you cannot remedy an organizational weakness without the active support of line management.

Training must therefore start *by bringing middle management on board*, beginning with the highest echelons to ensure that each management tier is involved in the training of those employees directly under its control.

1.3. Further Reinforcing an Organizational Strength

Having invented a new profession—comprising on-site service solutions (catering and facilities management) and motivational solutions (service vouchers and cards)—Sodexo achieves customer loyalty and satisfaction ratings well above those achieved by most of its direct competitors.

Nonetheless, for years, group management had believed that this strength needed to be further reinforced worldwide through specific action plans.

This was the purpose of the strategic project "Clients for Life," which has been the subject of numerous training initiatives.

Paradoxically, working on a strength is generally more readily accepted and understood by staff than working on a weakness.

In practice, strengths are already the object of attention and pride within the organization.

Training must simultaneously seek to *consolidate the basics* (even if they already seem to be under control), to *further improve team performance levels*, and to *systematically implement* good practice.

In a work that we have already quoted, Daniel Cable notes that *"the most difficult thing to imitate is something that requires discipline. If slimness and fitness could be bought like clothing, everyone would be slim and fit."*

In general, this all involves the intensive modeling of successful practices.

Thus, in Sodexo's case, all those initiatives contributing to customer loyalty were catalogued and described.

Once they have all benefited from some general training in this area, front-line Sodexo employees undergo annual training to perfect their performance in a particular aspect of customer loyalty. For example, the particular case of a change in the identity of the customer contact is the subject of a list of good practices and gives rise to dedicated training initiatives.

Exploiting the Best Aspects of a Company's Business Culture

Among the factors that explain L'Oréal's outstanding success over many decades, mention is often made of a certain number of values and patterns of behavior observed within that business.

For example, its managers excel in their ability *to create and sustain informal networks* outside functional and hierarchical structures, within an organization that is more "organic" than "mechanical."

Similarly, *passion for the product* and *professional sensitivity* are absolutely crucial elements of the L'Oréal culture.

As we saw in the introduction, culture is defined as the sum total of the strengths that an organization has accumulated over the years, to the extent of making them implicit priorities and practices, familiar to all.

Too often, the culture of a business is underused strategically. Indeed, as all magicians know, the human eye only notices things that move and ignores anything that doesn't move. Senior executives often possess a natural propensity for change that sometimes leads them to see only the negative aspects of an organization's culture.

Yet business culture constitutes a robust competitive advantage for them, as it is difficult to replicate rapidly.

Various studies have also demonstrated that, among the most long-lasting and most extraordinary business success stories, very few are associated with a sudden innovation or the eradication of a weakness.

On the contrary, those success stories are generally due to the continuous implementation of a single strategy over decades and to the continual reinforcement of a single competitive advantage. You need to tirelessly mine a single seam, provided that the seam has been well chosen.

Training has several roles to play here.

Firstly, it helps to *make the culture explicit.*

As a case in point, when L'Oréal's middle managers are trained in conducting annual staff assessment interviews—and particularly, mid-year career development interviews—they explicitly review the skills that underpin their business culture. For example, professional sensitivity and the ability to work in networks are precisely defined and illustrated by specific examples, in order that they may be duly evaluated and then reinforced in each individual.

Training also serves to ensure that each individual exploits *to the full* all the elements of the business culture. For example, while working in networks is a key feature of the group culture, training encourages each individual to actually use their network to pursue a greater number of more ambitious initiatives and to do so more effectively.

Lastly, training helps *to create new standards of excellence* in order to stay ahead of competitors, who are themselves making progress. It may therefore be appropriate to establish *innovation* teams in areas already seen as spheres of excellence, and also to dare to *create a vanguard* in-house by giving special training to an elite and exposing them to encounters with experts and business leaders *from outside their industry*.

Training Directed at Individual Progress

We have seen how a strategically important training program is bound to impact upon an organization at one or other stage in the dynamics of progress: unknown, weakness, strength, or culture.

If we move down to the level of the individual, this phenomenon operates in exactly the same way; we shall now examine what this means for training.

Let us take the example of a chain of high-street banks whose strategy involves promoting so-called *long-term* investment products such as pensions and life insurance in order, firstly, to consolidate its relationship with customers who have a high propensity to save and, secondly, to increase the loyalty of these customers to the bank.

As part of this approach, the bank wishes to systematically carry out an *annual investment review* with each customer from a particular segment of its client base.

In theory, some account managers have been carrying out such reviews for years, but using a wide range of methods that may or may not have been applied effectively. There are other account managers, however, who have yet to carry out an investment review with any of their staff.

The bank opts to roll out a dedicated training program for its 15,000 in-branch account managers so that the annual investment review will be applied in a systematic way and with exceptional effectiveness, as regards both sales of long-term investments and customer loyalty and satisfaction in the target segments.

This training program means very different things to different staff members, depending on whether the skill in question constitutes an unknown, a weakness, a strength, or an element of their professional culture.

Equipping a Staff Member with New Skills

For those account managers who have never before carried out an annual investment review, the bank's strategic project constitutes a major change.

Indeed, for them it is a case not merely of changing a habit or improving the way in which they do things, but of performing a series of tasks that they have never done before.

There are multiple risks of failure.

In fact, in such situations, some employees are tempted to *deny the benefits* of the new tasks requested: recognizing the relevance of annual investment reviews would equate, in their eyes, to admitting that until now they have lacked professionalism, compared to those of their colleagues who are adept at this commercial ritual. From the training phase, numerous objections can be anticipated, such as: "*This sort of approach doesn't suit customers like mine!*" "*It's all very well in theory, but in practice we haven't got the time for this!*" "*The method suggested is much too complicated!*"

Other account managers will happily accept the training but, faced with the fear of failure, they will tend to *avoid implementing it*. They will find a battery of excuses to justify the practical impossibility of carrying out the investment reviews requested—or to persuade others to carry them out. How can you really be sure of mastering the five preparatory phases, the twelve sections of the review interview, and the dozens of potential technical questions from customers? "*It seems easy when you're training, but when you're faced with a real-life customer, things are never like that!*"

Lastly, there are others who will try to put their training into practice right away, but who will tend to *give up at the first hurdle*. Why should you repeatedly expose yourself to failure in an area where others have accumulated experience that has enabled them to forge ahead?

To be effective, the training must pre-empt these various behavioral patterns by making each employee feel secure.

To achieve this, firstly it can place a high value on the employee's existing skills and help them to *make the link between the activity required and skills that they already possess*. For example, it may be appropriate to show that the annual investment review largely relies on interviewing techniques already used when opening an account.

In addition, training must *set the bar at an achievable level*. You do not move straight from the *unknown* to a *strength* without passing via the *weakness* box, that is to say a level of understanding temporarily lower than the average for good professionals in the field.

The key thing is not to encourage mediocrity, but to accept a phased progression that involves the mastery of ever more complex skills.

For example, this was the means by which a leading life insurance company spectacularly improved the performance levels of its young sales reps by training them in a *simplified sales method* covering a *limited range of products*. Once they were comfortable with this method, which generally took 2 years, those sales persons undertook further training in order to promote the entire product range and to master every facet of the company's sales methodology.

Training must then focus on *confidence building*, through the acquisition of simple professional actions, based on easily comprehensible and reproducible models. Coaching and repetition are particularly crucial here, as is recognition of the right to make mistakes when you first try to put training into practice.

Lastly, the training process must include *implementation support* on the first two or three occasions when an account manager prepares for, and then carries out an annual investment review, meaning that they must take "dual control" decisions with a manager or expert, in order to acquire the autonomy they need.

Helping an Employee to Remedy Weaknesses

Among the account managers employed by our bank, there are many who are used to carrying out investment reviews, but who have a very patchy understanding of the skills associated with that activity.

Some are held back by a *lack of technical knowledge*, perhaps about the product range or tax. Others *lack method*: they neglect certain essential stages of the preparation or the interview. Still others commit *behavioral errors*, such as failing to listen or else they lack self-confidence or open-mindedness, which can be enough to condemn an investment review to failure, even though it is conducted methodically by someone who is highly skilled from a technical perspective.

For individuals as for organizations, moving from a *weakness* to a *strength* is the most difficult phase in the dynamics of progress, as described at the start of this chapter.

In fact, employees are often unaware of their own *weaknesses*. Initially, discovering them tends to discourage those employees rather than to encourage them, especially if they involve a number of skills over the course of a training program.

Furthermore, a *weakness* is often connected to a set of habits that benefit the individual by offering a convenient comfort zone.

It is a fact that human beings will spontaneously tend to favor the short term: for example, having made a poor shot, an amateur tennis player will often prefer just to continue playing that way, rather than develop a different approach that will initially make things more difficult, but will eventually help improve their game in the long term.

In addition to the difficulties cited above about learning new skills, there is therefore the need to convince the employee to abandon their comfort zone for the discomfort of a new way of doing things.

This is the reason why *training programs that focus on correcting weaknesses often produce disappointing results.*

It is also why *training policies that are based too exclusively upon standards of competence, which might be impeccable on paper, are bound to disappoint*: by its very nature, remedying weaknesses is the most difficult exercise of all.

It is still true that remedying certain individual weaknesses is one of the standard objectives of any training program: either because the individual is seeking to perfect their own performance by eliminating vulnerabilities or because the interests of the organization demand it.

To achieve this effectively, the training program must help each employee to distinguish, among their weaknesses, those that are really *obstructing* the effective implementation of the strategy. It is to these—and these alone—that attention should be devoted.

Otherwise, it is more beneficial to help the employees to find solutions allowing them to neutralize their weaknesses. In certain cases, they can use stopgap measures, such as automatic reminders for a disorganized individual. In other cases, they need to work in harness with one or more partners: many great success stories (e.g., Microsoft, Apple, Accor Hotels) result from two complementary individuals working in harmony. In other circumstances, individuals need help to move to a role where their weaknesses will have no impact: for example, a more independent post for someone who struggles to relate to others, a less operational role for someone who finds it hard to take decisions.

Training must also *stimulate greater awareness without generating defensive behavior.*

In the case of our bank, putting the account manager in the shoes of a customer on the end of an ineffective investment review can act as a trigger. Humor—risky and definitely to be handled with care!—can also be helpful, as business role-play exercises in some training courses have often demonstrated.

Whatever the methods selected, the training must often highlight the negative consequences and risks attached to current operating methods in order to instill the desire in employees to change certain aspects of their working practices.

You then need to help the employee to make progress, by setting them *gradual and achievable targets.*

Many research projects in fact demonstrate the importance of getting the individual to focus on their progress in mastering a skill, and not on a distant performance target: this reduces the risk of the trainee becoming discouraged by a feeling of helplessness when confronted with problems that are too hard to handle.

Lastly, the training must *offer each staff member a protective framework* to help them to try out new working methods without fear of failure or ridicule.

Despite the fact that, in certain business cultures, people insist they want brutally honest feedback and ruthless criticism from the trainer and the group, a much more effective solution is to concentrate on confidence building.

At a fast-growing firm of brokers specializing in business insurance, the constant quest for excellence takes the form, for example, of requiring staff to undertake the following exercise: each rep is regularly invited to give a talk to a panel composed of two senior managers and an external consultant, in order to identify the areas in which they still have room for progress.

All the performances are video recorded. Once the panel's comments have been collected, the rep has a one-to-one discussion with the consultant, who "restabilizes" them, if necessary, then helps them to target a particular improvement selected as being important and achievable, encourages them, and gives them practical advice.

Further Reinforcing Each Employee's Strengths

Within our bank network, there are account managers for whom handling annual investment reviews is already a *strength* even before they undergo training.

Those reps are simultaneously using knowledge, methods, and appropriate behavior and they are performing the work associated with annual investment reviews to a satisfactory standard on a regular basis.

The questions arises, do they really need training?

When you ask a human resources director how training could benefit an employee, the response generally focuses on aspects already mentioned: "*provide new skills,*" "*cover skills gaps,*" "*help individuals to correct their weaknesses.*"

There are clearly areas in which this approach is fully justified.

For example, we can all agree that an airline pilot who struggles to *land* his plane correctly would be well advised to make it a priority to learn that skill, rather than to ceaselessly fine-tune his already perfect procedure for taxiing toward the runway. Likewise, any chain (including a chain of activities) is only as strong as its weakest link.

However, remedying the personnel failings has never been adequate to create or maintain a significant competitive advantage in any business.

In a competitive world, implementing a strategy requires the *creation of a culture of excellence*, at least in fields, roles, and occupations deemed to be essential to that competitive advantage.

Thus, a business whose strategy relies, for example, on innovation, must have *the best innovators*.

Similarly, our bank must push its top performers to *excel even more* in annual investment reviews and in the other activities associated with them. By continually raising its own performance levels, it will build a sustainable competitive advantage.

Not only that, but training an employee in one of their strengths is generally more effective than training them to correct a weakness.

In fact, none of the obstacles cited above (fear of failure, avoidance of new tasks, falling at the first hurdle, resistance to change, etc.) hinders the effectiveness of training in a strength: such training provides more motivation and self-esteem, as well as being easier, as the employee already possesses a solid grounding in this area.

Above and beyond all these points, the need for an entire organization to follow a single strategy does not result in having *average personnel* in every post; there are three reasons for this.

Firstly, experience shows that, considered individually, the best employees in any given profession never possess all the skills deemed essential for the fulfillment of their duties.

In theory, an account manager at a bank must, among other skills, be organized, must possess in-depth product knowledge, must listen to customers, and must be highly persuasive.

Yet within many banking corporations, you find that *none* of the best customer services representatives meet all four criteria. Some are completely disorganized, others have an imperfect knowledge of their product range; some fail to listen, while others express themselves hesitatingly. All of them make up for their failings in one area by possessing one or more exceptional *strengths* in others.

This means that high performance levels are much more closely associated with strengths than with the absence of weaknesses. That is why a business such as L'Oréal deliberately cultivates each employee's "rough edges."

Secondly, excellence requires *specialization*.

For example, it is obviously necessary for each player in a sports team to master the basics of the game and, if possible, even to be able to play several roles.

However, it is essential that the team should achieve a very high level of performance in every aspect of the game, which also requires intensive specialization by each individual. A good coach will encourage each player to identify those particular aspects of their play that they are best at and to devote a significant proportion of their training to cultivating those strengths.

In other words, on the whole *excellence is generally preferable to versatility.*

Thirdly, in the sphere of school education, it has long since been proven that a pupil who builds strengths in particular subjects gains in motivation and self-confidence, which rapidly impacts upon their results in their weaker subjects.

Likewise, by helping each employee to build up areas of excellence, you strengthen both the person and the organization.

In other words, and this is a central concept of this book: correcting weaknesses is essential, but *that training is much more effective when it concentrates on people's strengths.*

This has several major consequences for the managers of any training program.

Firstly, they must seek to identify each employee's strengths, whereas competency standards sometimes tend only to pinpoint shortcomings.

Secondly, they need to ensure that a sufficient proportion of training work, by time and budget, is allocated to training staff in their strengths.

Lastly, they must ensure that this is introduced into every training program: a course that merely draws the attention of individuals to their deficiencies has little chance of being effective.

You therefore need to resist the natural temptation of trainers (often encouraged by some trainees) to prove that they are adding value by continually highlighting the errors made by participants.

Helping Each Employee to Take Advantage of Their Professional Culture

For a few of our bank's account managers, the annual investment review is more than just a strength: it is an *asset* of long standing that they have fully assimilated. They can prepare for an investment review and carry it out without even glancing at the documents provided. They intuitively know how to quickly hone in on areas of uncertainty, on needs to be fulfilled, and on the right solutions to suggest.

In theory, they have already achieved an excellent standard in performing that task and it forms part of their professional *culture*.

So what could be the benefit in investing to train these people in a subject that they have already mastered?

A large volume of research indicates that for organizations the greatest potential progress in performance is to be found in *getting personnel to use their expertise in doing what they already know best.*

For example, the American organization Gallup put the following question to almost 200,000 employees working at almost 8,000 operating units for 36 major corporations: "*In your job, do you have the opportunity to do what you do best every day?*"

Overall, just one employee in five answered "Yes, absolutely." Yet within the top-performing units, that figure was almost one in two.[1]

Actually, the proportion of employees doing what they do best every day correlates to the performance of the unit to which they belong in respect of criteria as varied as productivity, customer satisfaction, and employee loyalty ratings.

Even more surprisingly, a *change* in the response to the question about using strengths enables us to predict a change in that organization's performance levels.

Incidentally, on average those employees who feel that they are able to do what they do best every day take fewer days off sick and have fewer accidents at work than the rest.

Yet the professional "culture" conceals other opportunities.

When Allied Breweries wanted to develop customer loyalty among drinkers at its public houses, it launched the "One Hundred Club," the aim of which was to reward bar staff who knew by heart the names and favorite drinks of 100 customers.

For some of the best bar staff, memorizing the identity and drinking habits of customers formed part of the work culture. Encouraged to cultivate this skill by the brewer's initiative, many of them quickly broke the hundred barrier. Allied Breweries was obliged to create a "Five Hundred

Club" and then even a "Three Thousand Club," whose first member was a bartender from the North of England, who knew the names and favorite drinks of three thousand customers by heart![2]

In fact, *when individuals are encouraged to make full use of skills that they have already mastered, they can achieve performance levels well above their normal standards.*

In this case, the role of training is therefore to help and encourage each employee to make the most of what they can do best.

This may mean helping them to identify new *situations* in which their skill can be expressed, to increase the *impact* of their actions, to *innovate more* in the way they work, or to *pass their professional culture on to others.*

Training must also, more specifically, teach *managers* to identify each employee's unique qualities.

Indeed, managers can only build excellent teams if they accept that each employee is endowed with different characteristics.

Recognizing each individual's identity requires the ability to accurately describe each of their professional fields of excellence, to specifically listen to each of them before taking a major decision on behalf of the team, to entrust different assignments to each person depending on their profiles and talents, to help each person to find their unique place within the team, and to build their own professional project.

Another skill to be developed in managers is for them to empathize with each member of staff. Ultimately, it is a case of seeing people as they are, praising their good qualities, being tolerant of their failings.

This empathy is essential as it allows you to identify the personal qualities behind the irritating failing: mark "splits hairs and gets bogged down in detail"; Claire systematically criticizes new ideas and finds all possible reasons why they "will never work"; Vijay always comes up with ideas for grandiose projects, taking absolutely no account of the cost, the risks, or the practical preconditions for success. A "talent spotting" leader will ask Vijay to come up with some ideas, Claire to identify their risks, and Mark to monitor the progress of each of the identified preconditions for success. Apart from this, such a leader will demand that each of them should develop high-level professional skills in complementary fields, depending upon their respective personal qualities.

In conclusion, any training project partly comprises new skills, at least for some of the employees concerned. It also allows them to correct errors and weaknesses.

However, it is not generally in this area that the most spectacular progress is made.

The strategy essentially involves reinforcing and exploiting strengths and developing a culture of excellence.

Training must therefore seek to allocate resources appropriately between these different purposes, depending upon the specific business context, and to adopt quite distinct objectives and methods.

It is true that there is another major difference: the one traditionally made between blue collar workers, who largely perform physical tasks, and white collar workers, who essentially handle data and documents.

Many believe that the training of the former is essentially manual, while that of the latter is predominantly intellectual.

The next chapter, entitled *An Animal Endowed with Reason and Emotions*, offers a radically different perspective.

Key Points to Remember

- The best strategies principally rely on a business's strength. Training must therefore allow for the systematic application of best practices.
- The culture of an organization is defined as the sum of all those strengths that have been so deeply assimilated that they have become natural instincts. This constitutes a competitive advantage that is difficult to replicate quickly. Training must ensure that each individual makes the most of the elements of the business culture.
- If you move down to the level of the individual, the trajectory of progress is exactly the same.
- When it is a case of equipping an employee with new skills, there are multiple risks of failure. You need to focus on confidence building.
- Helping an employee to correct a failing is even more difficult. Training must help the employee to identify those

of their weaknesses that really cause an obstruction and to try out new ways of working without fear of failure.

- Training must push each employee to further reinforce their strengths.
- For organizations, the greatest potential progress in performance is to be found in employees doing what they are able to do best.

Recommendations

The training connected to the implementation of our strategy …	Yes!	More or less …	Not yet
Is it designed *differently* according to whether the objective is to introduce a new practice into the organization, to correct a weakness, to reinforce a strength, or to exploit a feature of the business culture?			
When it consists in introducing a *new* practice into the organization, does it seek above all to build *confidence*?			
Does it therefore rely on *pioneers* with the responsibility for overseeing pilot operations?			
Does it rely on *models of success* built in-house?			
Does it seek to achieve *gradual* objectives, in order to win small victories?			
Do employees see it as going hand in hand with the *implementation* of the new activity?			
When it consists in correcting one of the organization's *weaknesses*, does it seek above all to overcome the *resistance to change*?			
Does it therefore put employees in a position where they *become aware* of what is at stake?			
Does it rely on "*positive deviants*" to prove the effectiveness of the practices presented?			
Does it provide the information required in order to *reassure* and often to *enlighten*?			
Is it organized so that each *middle management* tier is involved in training those employees directly under its control?			

When it involves further reinforcing one of the business's *strengths*, does it rely on the intensive *modeling* of best practices?			
Does it take particular care to consolidate the *basics*?			
Does it seek to ensure the *systematic* application of good practices?			
When it involves an area that is already well rooted in the business *culture*, does it seek to ensure that *the best possible use* is made of these elements?			
Does it therefore allow the culture to be made *explicit*?			
Does it help to create *new standards of excellence*?			
When it provides an employee with a *new skill*, is it a priority to try to build their *confidence*?			
Does it therefore place a high value on the employee's *assets*?			
Does it place the bar at an *achievable* level?			
Does it include *support* during implementation?			
When it involves an employee's *weakness*, does it principally seek to get them *to accept* change?			
Does it therefore specifically help the employee to identify which of their weaknesses really creates an *obstacle* and to accept the others?			
Does it help to encourage the employee to *become aware* of issues without generating *defensive* behavior?			
Does it set the employee *gradual* and *achievable* targets in order to reduce the risk of discouragement?			
Does it offer the employee a *protective framework* in order to try out new ways of working without fear of failure or ridicule?			
When it involves an employee's *strengths*, does it really seek to further *reinforce* them?			
Does it rely on a precise *knowledge* of each employee's strengths?			

(Continued)

(*Continued*)

Overall, does it include a sufficient commitment to training employees in their *strengths*, in terms of the *budget* share allocated?			
Does it explicitly make provision for each *trainer* to devote sufficient time to helping each employee to reinforce their *strengths*?			
Does it also specifically seek to help each employee to make *even better use* of *what they already do best*?			
Does it help each person to identify new *situations* in which their skills can be expressed, to increase the *impact* of their actions, to *innovate* more in their working practices, and to *pass their professional culture on to others*?			
Does it also, more specifically, seek to teach *managers* to identify the *unique qualities* of each of their members of staff?			

CHAPTER 4

An Animal Endowed with Reason and Emotions

The Difference Between Computers and Human Beings

When Nonce Paolini was appointed Chairman and Managing Director of the European broadcaster TF1 in July 2008, he immediately felt that he would have to make profound changes to group strategy.

Under the leadership of his predecessor, this pillar of French TV had enjoyed 20 uninterrupted years of dazzling success. Since privatization in 1987, TF1 had achieved audience ratings of about 40%, a level unparalleled in Europe. As a key player in the TV advertising market, TF1 had been in a position to dictate advertising rates for many years. Numerous diversification initiatives had expanded the group's range to new activities. In addition to Eurosport, TF1 now owned various specialist channels, production companies, web sites, e-commerce undertakings, and even a board-games manufacturer.

However, the market had begun to undergo a series of radical transformations. Firstly, digital terrestrial television was spreading like wildfire, offering viewers a choice of 18 free channels instead of the five available until then. Unlike some of its direct competitors, TF1 did not yet have a presence in this market sector. Secondly, a growing share of the advertising market was being colonized by Google and other new media, to the detriment of television. Lastly, the subprime

(*Continued*)

(*Continued*)

crisis, already affecting the United States, foreshadowed a financial and economic depression that was set to destabilize the world from October 2008.

While Paolini devoted the early months after his appointment to fine-tuning his diagnostics and adopting initial emergency measures, bad news piled up. The decline in TF1's audience share was accelerating and dragging down advertising revenues, while various diversified subsidiaries were accumulating losses. TF1 shares, which had been worth almost €30 in late 2007, had plunged down the stock market listings to just €5 by early 2009.

With his management team, Paolini drew up a new strategy designed to convert the group into a "360° information and entertainment business," active in all media, exploring every type of audience contact, and prioritizing competitiveness. This would involve constructing a new service offer, but above all it would require a new economic model. To have any chance of success, the strategy required profound changes to the way in which teams worked. They would need to decompartmentalize, pool resources, and rationalize.

Training was immediately identified as a key means for securing that success. The HR Director, Jean-Pierre Rousseau, asked Korda & Partners to train TF1's top 500 managers. But what exactly should they be trained in, to achieve the effective implementation of the strategy?

In this chapter, you will discover …
- *… that skills of many kinds are needed to deploy a strategy:*
  Possessing a technical command of management and knowledge of day-to-day tasks are simply not enough.
- *… that there are different individual profiles when it comes to learning processes:*
  People really are very different!
- *… how training can use universal languages to reach every employee.*

Skills of Many Kinds Are Needed
to Deploy a Strategy

In the previous chapter, we saw how the primary role of training is to help each employee develop a command of the actions essential to executing the strategy in their job. Along similar lines, we also saw how much can be done to improve the effectiveness of training.

However, nowadays effective strategy implementation requires a lot more than expertise in *execution*.

For example, Gary Hamel, an American named by the *Wall Street Journal* as the world's most influential management expert, has demonstrated that the degree of workforce involvement is crucial to corporate success.

He states that if an individual merely carries out orders, even quite willingly, many problems will remain unresolved. The corporation must allow its employees to demonstrate initiative, creativity, and even passion in their work.[1]

Apart from a command of the professional actions particular to each occupation, what are the different sorts of skills required for a strategy to succeed?

Learning to Think

In the case of TF1, as in many others, the implementation of a new strategy required the resolution of various problems that had never existed before.

If such problems could be anticipated and their solutions mapped out in advance, in theory it would be sufficient to train staff to carry out the instructions they are given. But that would be a mistake, for two reasons.

Firstly, in practice, organizational complexity and the pace of change make it impossible to predict, categorize, and process in advance the many problems which might occur during implementation.

Secondly, success in executing a strategy requires people to become *active* at every level of the organization. It is therefore necessary to *delegate some decision-making powers* to the various tiers in the organization.

Thus, it is not enough to train people to be good at following instructions: what is needed is a workforce that is able to *think*.

The world-renowned British doctor, philosopher, psychologist, and specialist in the cognitive sciences, Edward de Bono is the author of some fifty books on the methods of thinking.

He claims that most of the world's problems stem from the deficient intellectual methods that we use to resolve them.

In practice, when confronted with any issue, we all tend to form our opinions too quickly.

The greater our intellectual and cultural baggage, the more we tend to use our resources to defend our opinion, instead of seeking the best solutions to get to the root of a problem.

In response, de Bono calls for real training in thinking.[2]

In particular, he recommends that we should develop two particular skills: *parallel thinking* and *lateral thinking*.

Parallel thinking, as modeled by the famous "six hats" method, consists in dissociating the different perspectives of a given situation: distinguishing between facts and interpretations, between certainties and hypotheses, and between benefits and disadvantages.

The main obstacle to thought, he writes, is *confusion*. Such confusion afflicts an isolated individual grappling with a problem, and even more so a group of people debating an issue: when one participant makes a suggestion, another participant will often subject them immediately to criticism, either constructive or malicious. When one person tries to analyze a cause, another person will intervene to warn of the consequences! De Bono therefore calls on us to learn to think methodically.

Lateral thinking applies more to the creative quest for solutions.

Everyone will have noticed how, in reality, most innovative solutions do not arise from a rational deductive process: our best ideas come to us just when we are expecting them the least, often triggered by an external factor with no apparent connection to the subject. De Bono has therefore formalized a whole range of simple techniques that allow us to stimulate our creativity immediately.

For example, one technique is to pull a word at random from a dictionary and then elicit a series of suggestions spontaneously inspired by that word. Another is to work on an absurd or extreme hypothesis. For example, what would we do "if there was a total power failure" or "if we had zero budget."

Another example: as part of a training program, Danone offered a group of senior managers the opportunity to spend 2 days in Boston with a former criminal. Among other things, he told them how he had succeeded in running his gang from prison. This inspired a whole range of projects in the participants' minds, including remote management, the need to "liberate" employees and to encourage creativity.

Apart from learning methods, thinking is also improved by coaching.

Thus, in the case of TF1, as it was necessary to train managers in problem solving, each session featured various workshops tackling real-case work submitted by the course members.[3]

Developing the "Right" Brain

A former colleague of Al Gore when he was US Vice President, Daniel Pink, is arguably one of the most brilliant modern American thinkers.

Other then being author, speechwriter, and motivational speaker, he has also written several best-selling works of nonfiction, including *A Whole New Mind*, which many commentators see as one of the most important works of recent years.

The left side of our brain functions analytically and sequentially, whereas the right side is intuitive, inventive, and empathetic.

The left side can decipher a text, apply the instructions on a user manual or verify a procedure. The right side can recognize faces, read the emotions in another's expression, compose a work of art, or create a work of science fiction.

Pink notes that, until recently, the main skills required in our organizations have principally involved the left brain. He sees the *information age*, often said to have taken over from the *industrial age*, as marking the peak domination of the left brain.

However, he suggests that recent economic developments radically change the rules of the game, due to three strong trends.

Firstly, the growing power of Asia in skills terms, which, together with the boom in communications technologies, is facilitating the mass relocation not only of manufacturing but also, more significantly, of service-sector occupations: computer programming, accounting documentation, legal analysis, health diagnostics based on automated medical examinations, etc.

Secondly, there is the progress in intelligent tools allowing many previously manual operations to be automated. Certain software packages write software lines up to a thousand times quicker than the rate achieved by a top programmer. Others can automatically produce legal documents at a fraction of the cost charged by a lawyer. Very soon, any human task that can be accomplished more quickly and economically by a machine will be accomplished by a machine.

Thirdly, there is the abundance of material goods, especially in the United States, Japan, and Western Europe. The amount of waste being produced has reached unprecedented levels. In certain countries, such as the United States, the number of vehicle registrations exceeds the number of driving licenses. The furniture storage market alone is worth billions of pounds and is enjoying rapid growth. As a result, the principal aspirations of the consumer in the developed countries increasingly focus on the nonmaterial, revolving in particular around the quest for meaning, emotions, and relationships. The astonishing proliferation of video games, arts-based leisure, and social networks demonstrates this.

According to Daniel Pink, these changes presage the decline of most professions that rely mainly on the left brain and the mechanical application of procedures. This may be for three principal reasons: because they will be relocated, because they will be automated, or because they will no longer create sufficient value. He believes that the future therefore belongs to individuals capable of using their right brain. Hence, the subtitle of his book: *Why Right-Brainers Will Rule the Future?*

It is clear that many strategies require right-brain skills, yet few are covered by traditional training courses.

For example, building stronger customer relations is often dealt with solely from the perspective of processes, whereas the degree of *empathy* shown by sales and service staff is at least as crucial.

Likewise, managers' ability to "give meaning" is often crucial in the success of a strategy. Being able to explain a decision by telling a meaningful story rather than by listing "bullet points," convincing people about a new priority through inspiring imagery rather than simply giving orders, or raising morale with humor rather than anger are typical right-brain skills.

This all tallies with the research findings of Daniel Goleman, celebrated for having formulated the concept of *emotional intelligence*: the top-performing leaders stand out from the crowd through their right-brain skills, which have nothing whatsoever to do with their intelligence quotient (IQ).

To ensure the effective implementation of a strategy, training must therefore move beyond the restrictive boundaries of the left brain.

Businesses may indeed offer many personal development training courses. However, these generally remain disconnected from strategic challenges. A matter for regret!

In the case of TF1, one of the corporation's key challenges was to achieve cooperation between different institutions that had a poor knowledge or understanding of one another. After a series of exercises, a famous TV presenter made the following comment offscreen: "*This morning, I realized the constraints that our technical people face. In future, I will put myself in their shoes more and listen to them more: it is in all our interests to work together to find solutions rather than to play power games.*"

The Quest for "Self-Efficacy"

The Canadian, Albert Bandura, born in 1925, is one of the fathers of "Positive Psychology," a scientific movement that is less interested in treating diseases than with nurturing the full expression of people who already enjoy good health.

One of the major contributions of his research is the concept of self-efficacy,[4] defined as "an individual's belief in their own ability to organize and execute the actions necessary to handle situations which may arise." One might refer to the *feeling of competence* as opposed to competence itself.

This characteristic differs from the more general phenomenon of *self-esteem*: in a single individual, the feeling of competence can be high in relation to one activity and low in relation to another. For example, a barrister may consider himself to be an outstanding courtroom performer but useless at putting up shelves: his *self-efficacy* is low for Do It Yourself (DIY), but without his *self-esteem* necessarily being affected.

Bandura notes that this feeling of competence is crucial to an individual's behavior in a work context—and much more important than that person's actual level of competence.

Indeed, a high level of self-efficacy is necessary for a person to commit to a new task, rather than try to avoid it. Furthermore, this characteristic plays a big part in the degree of concentration and perseverance that an individual displays when confronted with difficulties.

In contrast, a lack of confidence in one's own abilities generates anxiety and "negative thinking that breeds failure."

Bandura therefore devoted years of research to identifying factors that generated self-efficacy. He identified four.

Firstly, there is *vicarious experience*, meaning that having been able to watch your peers successfully complete a task builds confidence: *"If they can do it, I must be able to do it, too!"*

Secondly, *social persuasion* plays a certain role. Congratulations and encouragement boost confidence to some extent, while negative comments sap such confidence to a devastating extent: *"They say that I've got the skills, so I must be able to do it!"*

Psychological state also influences self-efficacy: if someone suddenly has sweaty hands and a dry throat, they will often deduce that they are incapable of completing the task that they are about to perform. On the other hand, a euphoric state will boost their feelings of personal efficacy: *"I'm in a relaxed frame of mind, so the task is within my capabilities!"*

Lastly and most importantly, individuals assess their ability to perform a task according to their experience: do they or do they not feel that they have mastered a similar situation? Bandura explains that "experiences of success" play an essential role in building self-efficacy: *"I've already done this successfully, so I can do it again, no problem!"*

It will now be understood that training does not solely serve the purpose of providing people with the skills required to complete a task: it must also provide them with the level of *self-efficacy* essential to its accomplishment.

One of the fundamental reasons why so many training courses have disappointing impacts, in terms of strategy deployment will now become clear. It is not so much the level of the employees' skills that determines how new patterns of behavior can be implemented, but the level of confidence they have in their own abilities. Yet very few training packages fulfill the four criteria cited by Bandura. In particular, few indeed are those that offer employees real "experience of success."

Among the goals of a training course, it is therefore essential to set the objective of enabling each individual to accomplish the new task fully and successfully.

For example *a part of a* training workshop may be devoted to "two crucial minutes" in the success of a sales conversation. Each participant works on ensuring they successfully and confidently manage this crucial moment. With the help of a colleague playing the role of the customer, each person learns to apply their skills until they feel that they have fully succeeded.

More generally, the way in which the individual *interprets* their everyday working experiences is crucial to their future conduct.

Indeed, as demonstrated by another great American Positive Psychology expert, Martin Seligman, "causal attribution" is an essential factor in behavior.[5]

For an individual to persevere after a setback, they need to attribute this to specific temporary causes that were partly out of their control—and very definitely *not* to permanent, indeterminate, guilt-inducing, and ultimately dispiriting causes: "*I've failed because this particular circumstance worked against me and I was poorly prepared in one particular area, so next time I'll be able to do it.*"

Conversely, for that person to fully benefit from a success, they need to be able to attribute this not to a stroke of good luck, but to wider causes that are permanent and partly connected to their personal qualities and skills: "*I succeeded because tasks like this are made for me, so I'll be able to succeed again.*"

In sport, this constitutes one of the keys to effective coaching: helping the champion to interpret constructively every defeat and every victory.

In the business world, it should be the role of the manager to guide each staff member in interpreting the causes of their triumphs and their setbacks. This is a key factor in generating the optimism, self-confidence, courage, and perseverance that are necessary to achieve the new or difficult tasks required by the strategy.

Surprisingly, this topic is currently off the agenda of standard management training programs, both within universities and top training colleges, and at courses provided by leading training institutions.

Overall, *self-efficacy* is an indispensable condition for the specific implementation of training—and therefore for the effective deployment of a strategy.

It is therefore necessary for training itself to contribute, both through the teaching methods that it uses and through the educational grounding it gives to managers.

The Mysterious Luck Factor

In an excellent article published in 2009 by the *Harvard Business Review*,[6] two consultants from Deloitte Consulting and a lecturer from the University of Texas in Austin offered an original and worrying overview of the key factors in the success of business strategies.

Michael Raynor, Mumtaz Ahmed, and Andrew Henderson revealed the conclusions of a study covering more than 20,000 businesses monitored over a decade. The authors discovered that, among the 300 greatest success stories, a mere 25% did not attribute their success to pure luck. According to the researchers, most of these great successes merely benefited from opportunities that had been totally unforeseen a few years earlier.

These claims are probably excessive. However, there is no doubt that luck is a factor that enters into the deployment of a strategic initiative.

The researchers Robin Hogarth, Spyros Makridakis, and Anil Gaba also explored the role of luck in the outcome of decisions, notably in the world of business, and highlighted the importance of the "illusion of control."

Some celebrated experiments compared the predictive abilities, in relation to the stock market, of a financial analyst, an astrologist, and a monkey randomly throwing darts at numbers corresponding to various securities that were listed. Only the astrologist did worse than the financial analyst.

Why, then, do certain innovations peak at just the right moment, when so many others arrive too early or too late?

Why are certain commercial success stories facilitated by completely improbable personal connections outside working life?

Why are certain major projects disrupted by minor incidents, whereas others are facilitated by unexpected events?

Can we ultimately have any influence over the luck factor?

The work of the British Doctor of Psychology and Director of Research at the University of Hertfordshire, Richard Wiseman, casts a very interesting light on this issue.

Wiseman spent years trying to understand the factors determining consistent good and bad luck at the individual level.

He carried out extensive experiments, using thousands of volunteers who classified themselves in three categories: particularly lucky people, particularly unlucky people, and those enjoying a normal amount of luck. He subjected them to a range of tests and in-depth interviews. He was thereby able to demonstrate that the propensity to be lucky was not connected to any paranormal phenomenon, any more than it was to factors relating to IQ or to social origins. His research established that luck was directly connected to certain specific psychological and behavioral traits, which he listed and described in detail.

To prove the validity of his work, Richard Wiseman even created the "School of Luck" and demonstrated that particularly unlucky people could become luckier and more satisfied with their lives within a few weeks by methodically applying the principles identified in lucky individuals.

Among other things, Wiseman's research reveals the importance of developing and maintaining a vast network of personal relationships: in life, chatting frequently to strangers or staying in contact with former neighbors massively increases the probability that you will benefit from "strokes of luck."

Likewise, Wiseman demonstrated, for example, that differences in your openness to new experiences, your capacity to detect the opportunity in any constraint, or to learn lessons from setbacks play a decisive role in whether individuals are consistently lucky or unlucky.

When applied to the business world, these principles are just as relevant, if not more so. It is therefore possible to influence the luck factor in an organization by training individuals and teams to adopt a few simple but crucially important habits.

Not All Individuals Learn in the Same Way

We have seen that we need to guard against adopting too narrow an approach to the skills crucial to the deployment of a strategy. We shall now see that we also need to take account of the major differences that exist between individuals, in respect of their learning methods.

Gardner and Multiple Intelligences

The American psychologist Howard Gardner[7] is famous for having questioned the excessive reliance on aptitude tests to determine individual IQ.

Gardner demonstrated that such tests only measured two types of intelligence, which he respectively describes as *linguistic* and *logical* intelligence. These two types of ability are readily quantifiable and highly regarded by the school system, particularly for exams.

However, he claims that intelligence should be defined more widely as an "ability to solve problems [...] valued in at least one cultural setting or community." In addition, to the two above, he presents another six forms of intelligence.

Spatial intelligence is the ability to grasp vast areas or localized spatial arrangements. Among other things, this skill allows you to understand a labyrinth. It is also useful to chess players.

Musical intelligence allows you to perceive and create sound structures and helps you to master foreign languages.

Bodily-kinesthetic intelligence enables you to use your body to resolve problems, as in the case of a chiropractor or a mountaineer.

Naturalistic intelligence is a skill found in great hunters as well as top botanists.

Interpersonal intelligence, already cited among the "right brain" skills, is a particularly crucial form of intelligence among leaders, as seen in Goleman's research, quoted above. It is also essential in customer relations and in all those professions requiring teamwork.

Intrapersonal intelligence is a skill that helps you to stand back from events and to display lucidity and objectivity.

If we accept, as Gardner does, that there are at least eight forms of intelligence, we must immediately pose the following question: How should training adapt to different personal profiles?

Multiple Intelligences and Training Methods

Based on the modes of intelligence defined by Howard Gardner, Bruce Campbell worked to define the training methods best suited to different learner profiles.[8]

He claims that people endowed with *linguistic intelligence* learn most effectively by listening, reading, taking notes, and participating in discussions.

To perfect a foreign language, for example, such individuals must concentrate on reading books and magazines, listening to news and songs on the radio, or writing letters to a correspondent.

Logical intelligence is better suited to learning through problem-solving exercises, such as crosswords or Scrabble.

Spatial intelligence involves the ability to visualize diagrams and graphics. To learn a foreign language, it may be useful to employ color coding to distinguish the various functions of words in a sentence, or graphics to explain phrasal structure.

For people with a gift for *musical* intelligence, it is necessary to associate sounds or music with the items to be learned. For a foreign language, listening or composing songs is ideal.

Bodily intelligence is perfectly suited to the acquisition of skills in manual work. It may seem more difficult to use in the assimilation of abstract data, but role playing or even choreographic exercises associated with concepts—or words and expressions, in the case of a foreign language— promote learning and retention.

Naturalistic intelligence is suited to learning through observation, the classification of items observed, and the analysis of the relationships between those items. Exercises involving the description of images or the preparation of a presentation in a foreign language are well suited to progress in this area.

Interpersonal intelligence is best exploited by employing small-group learning methods. To learn languages, board games and group exercises (e.g., rehearsing a play) are highly suitable.

Lastly, people endowed with great *intrapersonal intelligence* benefit most from self-evaluation tasks at different stages of a training course. During a foreign language lesson, for example, it will be useful for them to practice role playing and exercises allowing them to express or to describe their emotions.

Learning Styles: Many Theories, One Certainty

Gardner and Campbell's approach has been heavily criticized for failing to provide convincing evidence from experiments using these methods carried out in a school environment.

Other researchers have addressed the specific issue of different learning styles, regardless of forms of intelligence.

Our goal here is not to describe all their theories in detail, but to make the reader aware of the scale of the differences between individuals when it comes to methods of acquiring skills.

The research of the New Zealander Neil Fleming demonstrates that some people learn through sight, others by listening, yet others through reading and writing, while others again do so by learning through their own personal experiences.

An American named David Kolb believes that experimentation is at the heart of learning. He distinguishes between four learning profiles: *convergers* tend to conceptualize and then to actively experiment, *divergers* begin by acting and then draw lessons from this, *assimilators* conceptualize, but then observe and reflect, *accommodators* are action focused, that is, they understand by doing things.

His colleagues Peter Honey and Alan Mumford have taken this model further.

According to them, the *activist* style is characterized by a taste for action and an enthusiasm for anything new. *Reflectors* like to analyze things in detail and to take stock. In contrast, those preferring to act as *theorists* organize their observations in order to use logical connections to deduce generally applicable principles from those observations. Lastly, *pragmatists* like to find solutions to specific problems and to put ideas into practice.

When it comes to learning, these four styles are seen as *preferences*. They are not fixed and individuals may change their ways of learning.

Anthony Gregorc puts forward another model, based on the existence of perceptions that are concrete or abstract, and sequential or random. He identifies four types of learning depending on the dominant perceptions in different categories of people.

People who favor *concrete and sequential* perceptions learn based on precise facts, in logical stages and through pragmatic implementation. Those who have a *concrete and random* profile learn by experimenting and by working alone to solve problems, ideally in a competitive environment. Profiles favoring *abstract and sequential* perceptions learn through analysis and discussion with experts. Individuals with an *abstract and random* profile generally learn through group activities defined by broad and flexible instructions.

After this overview of some different approaches, just one thing is clear: individuals do not all learn in the same way.

Trompenaars & Hampden-Turner and Cultural Models

A Dutchman named Fons Trompenaars and his British colleague Charles Hampden-Turner, both highly respected academics, came together to pursue research and to produce publications that now set the benchmark for the understanding of cultural differences.[9]

These partly explain the difficulties raised by the deployment of a strategy within an international corporation, which by definition comprises human groups that vary widely from one another due to the values and codes of behavior created by their local environment.

Among the seven dimensions to their cultural model, three are of particular relevance when it comes to strategic training.

For example, it has been established that Anglo-American cultures generally bear the hallmark of *universalism*: rules takes precedence over interpersonal relationships.

In other cultures, categorized by researchers as *particularist*, which are to be found both in Spain and in many Asian countries, it is individual relationships that count.

This helps explain the problems encountered by certain American corporations that have asked their employees worldwide to inform on colleagues who break their organization's ethical or safety rules: something that comes naturally in one environment is unthinkable in another.

When it comes to training, of course, an approach highlighting rules and general principles will therefore produce very mixed results depending on the cultural context.

Likewise, human societies are characterized by different degrees of *individualism* or *communitarianism*, which shape behavior at work, but also during training. Thus, Japanese staff will sometimes struggle to adopt a personal stance on a subject or circumstance, particularly if they have to stand out from the opinion of the group. In contrast, they will generally show immense loyalty to the deployment of a work program to which their entire corporation is committed.

The issue of *status* is also addressed quite differently according to geographical location. In the Scandinavian countries, for example, personal status depends upon merit; it can vary according to the circumstances and has only a weak impact upon the nature of relationships between individuals. In other countries, such as Venezuela, Indonesia, or even China, status is predominantly acquired through personal characteristics such as age, gender, family origins, and relational networks.

Must training therefore systematically adapt to each of the countries in which it is provided? No, but it needs at least to identify the specific cultural obstacles to be taken into account in particular areas where the corporation operates.

For Large-Scale Training, You Need to Use Universal Languages

When preparing staff for the deployment of a strategy, we have seen that training should extend well beyond the technical skills directly necessary for the accomplishment of the tasks involved: employees really do have to develop their ability to *think* effectively in order to solve new problems, to mobilize their *right brain* in order to display empathy and sensitivity, to reinforce their *self-efficacy*, and to influence the luck factor insofar as possible.

We have also seen that within a single organization there are individuals who differ profoundly from one another in their forms of intelligence, their cultural environment, and their learning styles.

To deal with the training of large numbers of people, we therefore have no option but to adopt *universal languages*. It can be argued that there are three such languages these days: stories, play, and personal experience.

Telling Stories

As the founder of the Institute for Learning Sciences in Chicago, Roger Schank is seen as one of the leading world experts on artificial intelligence and the theory of learning. According to him, *"humans aren't wired to understand logic, they're wired to grasp stories."*

Indeed, people's love of stories is universal. Stories and legends have always been an essential tool for the transmission of cultures, religious beliefs, and social mores. Despite the development of alternative forms of leisure, cinema continues to fascinate millions of people and to generate considerable income. On a more universal level, the art of telling or understanding stories underpins numerous activities: advertising, sales, the medical professions, etc. According to some estimates, these activities represent a third of the gross domestic product of the developed world.

When Muhammad Yunus, the Nobel Peace Prize winning inventor of microcredit, wanted to convince business leaders to contribute to his work, he began by recounting the story of Sufia Begum, who was unable to drag her family out of poverty because of the difficulty of obtaining credit, despite working hard in her village in Bangladesh to make bamboo stools. At the end of his speech, the audience was on its feet and the emotion was tangible throughout the hall.

Thus, a business strategy can only really win personal commitment when it is delivered in the form of a story. How can we discuss the Hewlett-Packard story without first mentioning the garage in which Bill Hewlett and Dave Packard began their adventure in 1938? A story allows everyone to identify the *meaning*, to identify the current moment as a logical extension of the past, and to grasp the challenges of the next chapter that is to be written, whether that involves turning round a dangerous situation or setting out on the conquest of glorious new horizons.

Barack Obama's famous acceptance speech, during which he briefly looked back over a century of American history through the eyes of a black woman voter who had just voted in Atlanta at the age of 106, epitomizes this: despite it having been a bitterly disputed election night that speech, which summed up the new President's ambitions and concluded with the slogan "Yes, We Can!," won almost unanimous approval nationwide and across the world.

In training, stories also act as an absolutely central and universal vector of transmission.

The best trainers are well aware of this: they have always interspersed their sessions with personal anecdotes and amusing examples that capture the attention and are easy to remember.

In the modern world, stories are of even more crucial importance. Indeed, the key role of a trainer is no longer to *provide information* as that is generally available online! Information only produces an impact if it is provided in a way that *provides meaning* and stimulates *emotion*. In a few words, a story encapsulates an item of information, a context (providing meaning), and an element of surprise (providing emotion).

If very large numbers of people are being trained to deploy a strategy, the problem with "classroom" training is that a large number of trainers are needed. Now, it is difficult for a trainer to use someone else's personal stories without losing the authenticity and spontaneity of that account. Furthermore, if each trainer opts to tell their own stories, it is impossible to guarantee the consistency and relevance of the many different accounts to which the various employees will be exposed.

That is why storytelling in training is adopting new forms.

Firstly, *lectures* are making a comeback in training programs. This method was disparaged for a long time, justifiably so in certain cases, as it placed trainees in a passive situation and did not allow them to work deeply on their specific context. These days, lectures are used as a part of a multimodal journey to allow staff members to *collectively listen to a single story*, to feel the same emotions, and to share the same references. The lecturer is no longer expected to commentate on slides displaying words and figures, but to offer their personal experience, to describe pivotal moments in their own journey, and to share their "reading" of events.

Secondly, despite hardly being an innovatory technique, the use of *video* is more and more widespread: accessible online, inserted into e-learning modules, or shown in a training room, a short video allows trainees to listen to the personal account of a senior executive, the anecdotal experience of a colleague or an external example recounted by an expert. As it can be used more flexibly than a lecture, a video has the great merit of ensuring that the same account is delivered in the same way and with the same level of quality to all employees concerned.

Lastly, there is no doubt that the *symbolic anecdote* constitutes the most powerful way of using a story.

One day, a retired couple arrived at the Southwest Airlines check-in counter at Dallas Airport, accompanied by a large, friendly dog on a lead.

The airline check-in assistant was astonished to see the dog there: "You do know that you cannot take that dog on board with you, don't you?"

The couple was astonished: "Our dog goes everywhere with us! We're going on holiday to see our grandchildren. It's the first time we've ever flown and nobody warned us that it was impossible to take our dog!"

The check-in assistant expressed regret, but international regulations prevented her from allowing the dog on board. Check-in was on the point of closing and she needed to know whether the couple wanted to board the flight or not.

The woman burst into tears, sobbing: "We can't abandon our dog—and we've been dreaming about this holiday …"

The employee then asked: "How long are you going for?"

"Two weeks," the woman replied.

The clerk paused for thought and then murmured: "Listen, I love dogs. I'll take yours home with me. He'll be waiting for you when you disembark from your return flight."

That was the end of the story, but the start of a legend.

That story did the rounds of Southwest Airlines. Various senior executives picked up on it and repeated it. During induction training every course member would hear it. One day, in their turn, many of them would retell the story to a friend or a customer. No doubt that story did more for training in the customer service for which Southwest is known than any number of lectures and teaching exercises!

The ex-boss of Sony Pictures, PolyGram, and Columbia Pictures, and producer of films such as "Rain Man," "Batman," and "The Color Purple," Peter Gruber lectures at UCLA. He explains that while the art of storytelling may have changed little over the centuries, it is an art that has become an essential skill within organizations. He claims that the factual accuracy of the account is secondary: what matters is the sincerity of the narrator's convictions.

Playing Games

The importance of play in training has long been known, but it is sometimes poorly understood: "*This course concerns a serious subject of strategic importance! Don't you risk devaluing the subject by treating it all as a game?*" "*Are we going to treat our employees like children?*" "*Do we have to waste time on silly games, when we could be studying our documents in depth?*"

A large volume of scientific research, ranging from molecular biology to studies on animal behavior, via neuropsychology and cognitive psychology, proves the importance and universality of play in skills development.

Like stories, play is indeed a universal language.

In the first place, it constitutes a powerful factor in winning attention and engagement.

Divide people into three groups and ask them to consider a single problem simultaneously: they will probably do so reluctantly and with patchy commitment.

Whatever country you are in, if you call those groups "teams," announce a strict time limit, state that referees will allocate points to the best team and impose a penalty on the worst, then the work will be done at top speed and with much quality and commitment all around.

Play also allows you to make personal challenges less dramatic and to take the heat out of certain discussions. According to the work of Stuart Brown, the psychiatrist, researcher, and director of the National Institute for Play, "play creates a feeling of belonging and cooperation."

Lastly, it allows people to contribute *positive emotions* that promote a desire to act at the end of the training program.

Naturally, the play must have a precise educational objective and form must not take precedence over substance.

In the case of TF1, during the initial days of seminars for the training of middle and senior managers, fifty participants were organized into nine teams, each representing a Formula 1 stable. The "Formula 1 on TF1" trailers were played in the training room before each race. All those present got involved, like a cluster of mechanics around a racing car, resolving the practical issues put before them.

However, play does not merely involve competition: it also provides an opportunity to unleash humor and creativity. Thus, when the participants were invited to draw frescos, to compose songs or to act out sketches illustrating the implementation of the strategy, something very profound occurred: those people made a personal commitment to the strategy in their "hearts" as well as in their minds.

In conclusion, play is a powerful means of *encouraging learning*, especially when it is combined with storytelling.

For example, a major engineering and construction firm decided to make environmental protection a central plank of its strategy. The first phase involved ensuring that all its 35,000 employees were familiar with a *green economy glossary*. Given the cost involved, it was impossible to organize classroom training. How, therefore, were they to encourage tens of thousands of people, scattered across three continents and sometimes overloaded with work to learn all this new vocabulary?

The firm decided to use a "serious game," "*L'expertise dans la peau*" ("The Expert Within"): the employee is plunged into a universe reminiscent of suspense-based American TV series such as "24." With a mysterious organization on their trail, they had a limited amount of time to foil a plot endangering the global economy. The green economics terms constituted the passwords they needed in order to complete their mission. The music boomed out, the commentaries were read by famous actors—and the suspense was very real.

For the senior management teams from the various countries and regions, self-tuition was insufficient: they needed to get the managers working together to draw up action plans.

Once again, they adopted a game-based format, led by a consultant, at expanded management committee sessions within each national subsidiary, where the senior managers were invited to address the subject of the green economy.

Some were initially reticent when faced with shouldering the extra burden of the "Green Economy" work, but they *took to the game* like ducks to water: there were bursts of laughter and enthusiasm, and in a highly stimulating atmosphere those senior managers took the training on board and produced their action plan.

Real-Life Experiences

Apart from their different cultures, languages, forms of intelligence, and learning styles, human beings learn through their *emotions*: the fear or pain felt after careless behavior provides a sharper, longer-lasting lesson than words alone.

In addition and most importantly, unlike words, emotions push us to *act*.

Indeed, as the neurologist and neuropsychiatrist Richard Restak has demonstrated, the neocortex (the part of the brain capable of analyzing language) does not lead us to act; it distances us from the action. It is the limbic brain, as the seat of our emotions, which determines our conduct.

Thus, putting people in a situation where they *live through experiences* is a powerful method of training in any environment and for any individual.

For example, putting yourself in your customer's shoes for a few hours—or even just a few minutes—is often worth more than all the talk, images, and discussions you can find.

In conclusion to this chapter, corporations still have a lot to do in order to fully exploit each employee's potential.

They all do now understand that you cannot reduce an individual to a pair of hands, whatever their role within the business is. However, an individual undergoing training is still too often reduced to no more than a linear, rational left brain.

Yet any individual can contribute to the achievement of a strategy by adapting to situations, taking initiatives, cooperating with others, and displaying creativity. Individuals need training in every aspect of these skills, however.

Six months after its middle management training operation, TF1 commissioned an independent body to conduct an in-house survey into staff opinions and the working atmosphere among all its employees, who expressed their views anonymously.

Despite the depth of the crisis and the scale of the changes, 85% of them claimed to understand the new strategy and to be confident about their employer's future.

Those figures were even higher among managers, 90% of whom supported the strategy. That would have been unthinkable just a few months earlier.

After 1 year, the corporation announced a 14% rise in turnover, the tripling of operating profits, and a 51% rise in net profit.

Did training contribute to those results?

TF1 CEO, Nonce Paolini, is clear: "*in record time, it enabled five hundred managers to go back to their desks with a clear vision of the strategy and conduct to be adopted during that crisis. More than a training program, it was a revelation.*"

At this stage, we have mentioned the major improvements that are within the reach of those responsible for large-scale training projects within traditional organizations that use traditional technical resources.

The next chapter, entitled *Web Communities and Training*, will take us into the fascinating world of collaborative tools and reveal new aspects to knowledge sharing.

Key Points to Remember

- The application of strategy requires you to solve new problems. It is therefore often useful to train your employees to think.
- Recent economic developments require us to rapidly reinforce our right-brain skills, notably emotional intelligence.
- Apart from skills, training must provide people with a "feeling of competence."
- It is possible to help people to have a positive influence on "the element of luck" when rolling out a strategy.
- Not all individuals learn in the same way; there are eight forms of intelligence, different learning profiles, and different national and local cultures.
- To train large numbers of people, you need to employ universal languages: stories, play, and experiences.

Recommendations

The training connected to the implementation of our strategy ...	Yes!	More or less ...	Not yet
Does it help employees to apply solutions, in addition to solving new problems *for themselves*?			
Does it highlight "right-brain" skills (e.g., emotional intelligence, creativity) as much as "left-brain" skills?			
Does it allow every employee to specifically realize that what they are being asked to do is perfectly *feasible*?			
Does it help to build each employee's confidence, through encouragement and *praise*?			
Does it help to build each employee's confidence by associating new practices with a positive *physiological and emotional state*?			
Does it help to build each employee's confidence by allowing them to gain personal experience of *mastering* the skills expected of them?			
Is it promoted and added to by *middle managers* who know how to boost everyone's *confidence*?			
Does it take account of *the luck factor* and the way in which employees can influence it?			
Does it employ a range of educational methods likely to suit different *forms of intelligence* and different *learning profiles*?			
Does it take account of local *cultural* contexts which could affect its perception and implementation?			
Does it use *storytelling* as an essential vector for the transmission of messages, thereby delivering stories of high quality, both in substance and in form?			
Does it make extensive use of various forms of play, to stimulate attention, cooperation, and the desire to act?			
Does it systematically provide each employee with *real-life experiences* that are vivid and instructive?			

CHAPTER 5

Web Communities and Training

The Era When Everyone Helped Everyone Else

The Consumer Healthcare Division of the GlaxoSmithKline Group accounts for a turnover of €4bn, with R&D and marketing teams spread across the globe working on a wide range of brands.

In 2004, to ensure continuous growth in a constantly changing environment, senior executives decided to concentrate the group's product development and sales support work on major global initiatives. The decision was taken to centralize R&D and marketing for its leading global brands within a unit christened *The Future Group*. Today based at the group's global headquarters (HQ), this team comprises top executives. They compare ideas on a daily basis, continuously learn from contact with their peers, and produce some remarkable work that is constantly moving forward.

The group's initiation, however, caused problems for the company's staff in other parts of the world. Many far-flung R&D and marketing executives became frustrated. Limited to handling lesser brands, they felt as if they were second-class employees. They were concerned they would not continue to develop their skills.

The corporation therefore created the *Spark Network*. This was a network of 50 employees working on local markets in every corner of the world. The members were not "volunteers"; they were selected by regional CEOs from among their most creative and talented employees. The members of this network began to work together and

(*Continued*)

(*Continued*)

develop joint projects on a global level, thanks to the intensive use of web tools, such as teleconferencing, blogs, instant messaging, and collaborative web sites.

Some physical meetings were then introduced into the mix. Firstly, five members of the *Spark Network* participated in each *Future Group* meeting with the aim of learning and then informing the rest of the network. Next, an inaugural *Spark Network* world convention was staged in London. Organized in teams as a series of competing agencies, the members developed specific proposals for action and received instant feedback from the senior executives and experts present.

Within the network, training was intense and wide ranging. Staff learned varying methods of innovation, marketing metrics, and the power of storytelling when applied to brands. Each member of the *Spark Network* was then asked to lead a mission within their own region of the world—to form a similar community revolving around a major local brand.

A few years after its launch, the corporation recognized the great importance of the *Spark Network* in the success of its new strategy. Although geographically isolated, its members developed new skills and acquired a common culture that was more internationally focused than before. Their commitment to serve the group had never been so powerful.

This is the magic of *communities* and the new generation of *collaborative tools*.

In this chapter, you will discover …
- … *the extent to which communities and collaborative tools have become crucial in deploying strategic initiatives.*
- … *that a new collaborative business model is in the process of transforming organizations … and reinventing training.*

The Importance of Communities to the Deployment of a Strategy

There is a fundamental need for organizations to develop their "community" dimension. Recent history tells of the growing power of this concept.

Granovetter and the "Strength of Weak Ties"

In 1973, an American sociologist named Mark Granovetter, a Stanford professor, published an article[1] that was to revolutionize the way in which we analyze human groups, particularly in the workplace.

Until then, specialists had focused almost exclusively on small groups of people among whom strong ties had been established. For example, in the 1930s, the celebrated works of the Australian Elton Mayo essentially concentrated on a few workshops within the Hawthorne Electrical Works. Each group was studied in isolation. Among those people who saw each other every day "human relations" became established and these were observed, analyzed, and interpreted. This work was relevant, useful, and ultimately invaluable.

Yet Granovetter saw a much wider picture, with his theory of the "strength of weak ties (SWT).

He claimed that every individual belonged to two different groups. Firstly, there was a group of close acquaintances. Within this group, there were numerous ties between the different people surrounding an individual. Secondly, there was a much larger group. More specifically, that same person and *all* the people he or she knew constituted a low-density network, within which many people did not know one another.

Granovetter demonstrates that *weak ties* are of the utmost importance to personal development and the functioning of a human society. Indeed, it is these weak ties that allow bridges to be built between different small groups of close acquaintances. This is how information is passed on, how a common culture develops, and how movements and projects are created and extended.

Granovetter's article caused quite a stir: over the next 40 years or so, he was quoted more than 7,000 times in other scientific publications worldwide.

We can see the crucial importance of these "weak ties" in the implementation of a strategy within a large organization and, more specifically, in the expansion of the skills necessary to its implementation.

Ronald Burt and "Structural Holes"

As Professor of Sociology and Strategy at Chicago University, Ronald Burt added to Granovetter's work by highlighting the importance of filling "structural holes" that hinder the circulation of knowledge within a human society.

In particular, he cited a study conducted among security guards. He asked them how many people they knew in twenty different occupations. It seems that the more that they had the opportunity for contact in a variety of environments, the broader their knowledge of sport, art, literature, restaurants, and professional journals!

However, within any group there are many "structural holes" to be plugged.

We can therefore understand how the expansion of skills, including those associated with the deployment of a strategy can be hindered by these structural holes. When people do not know one another, they cannot habitually discuss their different fields of knowledge in order to make mutual progress.

Robin Dunbar and His "Number"

The British anthropologist and Oxford professor, Robin Dunbar, is also a biologist specializing in the evolution of species.[2]

Among the notable scientific writings for which he is known is a major discovery known as "Dunbar's number."

In the early 1990s, he began by comparing the size of the neocortex among various categories of primate and the number of individuals belonging to social groups. To his surprise, he found that there was a clear proportional connection. The larger the neocortex, the better the animal was able to handle a large number of relationships with its fellow creatures, including different degrees of closeness, different hierarchical levels, and different social roles.

Dunbar then wondered about the consequences for human beings of this finding. He first advanced and then studied the hypothesis that man's ability to handle relationships was also quantitatively limited by the size of his neocortex. Dunbar claimed that each of us is capable of grasping and dealing properly with a personal network of about 150 people. This is "Dunbar's number."

When we consider the size of major corporations today, we are immediately aware that Dunbar's number poses significant problems.

Given the number of interconnections necessary to deploy a strategy and to spread the skills associated with it, it is obvious that we need to find new methods of exceeding that limit, but is that truly feasible?

Mintzberg and "Communityship"

Henry Mintzberg, a Professor of Management Sciences from Montreal, is one of the most eminent management "gurus" of the last 40 years. However, it was not until 2006 that he opened the eyes of the business world to a concept that was to revolutionize organizations.[3]

In a series of brilliant articles, Mintzberg attacked the excessive glorification of *leadership*. He claimed that too much *leadership* led to too much *followership*, especially in very large corporations where employees struggled to feel any recognition.

He recognized that senior executives were increasingly vocal in claiming that their corporations had a vocation for *citizenship*. Yet Mintzberg felt that those top executives were missing the point; they needed to get down from their pedestals and devote their time to creating *a sense of community* within their own organizations. He saw communities as structured around collective goals, shared values, and strong relationships, which cemented an organization's common culture, and which was essential to the effective and sustainable implementation of a strategy.

He even suggested a new word, communityship, which he said could take its place somewhere between *leadership* and *citizenship*.

In short, to train their employees to roll out their strategy, it is essential that major corporations exploit *weak ties*, fill *structural holes*, exceed *Dunbar's number*, and give each employee the feeling that they belong to a *community*. But how exactly is this to be achieved?

This is where the Web 2.0 technological revolution comes in, as it takes what had previously been a utopian dream and suddenly makes it a possibility.

How Web 2.0 Is Transforming Organizations

First used in 2005 by the visionary Irish online publisher, Tim O'Reilly, the term Web 2.0 is now in common parlance and is associated with community web sites such as Facebook and YouTube.

This is certainly not the first revolution associated with information technology. The mass installation of computers within corporations during the 1970s, the advent of microcomputing in the 1980s, the appearance of email in the 1990s, and then the everyday use of the first web tools in the 2000s each brought changes to corporations.

But this is only the beginning!

Web 2.0 is more than just a name, but neither is it merely a relabeling of existing software. It not only represents the birth of a new generation of tools but also of functions and systems that are already impacting on our private lives, our organizations, and society in general, as was once the case with the invention of telephone or television.

Understanding the Nature of Web 2.0

From 2005, Tim O'Reilly highlighted the characteristics of those internet companies that had not only survived the bursting of the "dotcom" bubble in 2000 but were also actually prospering on the web.

Those corporations (Google, eBay, Wikipedia, and YouTube) shared the characteristic that they drew their *content* from *users*, unlike traditional sites that place products or information at the disposal of essentially passive web surfers.

The consequence O'Reilly immediately recognized was that, for each of these corporations, the more the number of users grew, the more the network effect intensified, thereby increasing the value of the service provided.

Harvard Professor and Web 2.0 specialist, Andrew McAfee then highlighted the three essential characteristics of Web 2.0.

Firstly, communication between people no longer only takes place through *channels* (inaccessible to third parties) but via *platforms* on which contributions can be viewed by anyone in the world and consulted at any time. This is the difference between a mobile phone conversation, or even an exchange of text messages, and a blog, for example.

Secondly, whereas traditional IT tools (enterprise resource planning, content management system, etc., and even "knowledge management" tools) impose heavy constraints on users as regards the nature and format of the information to be input, 2.0 tools are characterized by the absence of structural and procedural constraints.

This is how, for example, the founders of Wikipedia succeeded in building an encyclopedia containing 11m articles, more immediately up to date than the celebrated Encyclopaedia Britannica. Yet their first online encyclopedia, Nupedia, required a much heavier editing and inspection process: after 18 months of work, it contained just 12 articles.

Lastly, 2.0 tools do not need to be classified in advance and they offer mechanisms that allow a structure to emerge organically.

Thus, Google was the first search engine to view the web as a community within which members referenced one another through hypertext links and used those links to establish classifications relevant to all other users.

In short, according to McAfee, Web 2.0 tools are *social platforms that allow people to form online communities and to collaborate freely in various ways, making contributions and interactions visible and persistent over time, and allowing information to be gradually structured for greater ease of access.*

These tools generally allow users to search (usually via keywords and the uploading of content such as text, photos, videos, and links), to categorize content that is already online (the technique known as "tagging") and to send alerts to indicate when some relevant information has just been uploaded.

McAfee states that Web 2.0 is already creating "Enterprise 2.0," a term that characterizes any organization using these new tools to achieve its goals.

From Web 2.0 to Enterprise 2.0

As a global networking leader with a turnover of $40bn and a workforce of 63,000, Cisco is directly involved in the development of the web.

For several decades, its CEO, John Chambers, has been one of the most charismatic and visionary figures in the technology industry, alongside Steve Jobs and Bill Gates.

He is now convinced that *"with the proliferation of collaborative Web 2.0 technologies, the [Cisco] network continues to evolve from the plumbing of the internet—providing connectivity—to the platform that will change the way in which we work, live, learn and play."*

Obsessed by the desire to grasp new market opportunities, Chambers very quickly realized that Web 2.0 could help his own corporation to become more efficient. Naturally, Cisco has been one of the first players in the market to experiment successfully with and implement such technologies on its own account.

He explains that, from 2003, he established a "structure" and a "discipline" that allowed the corporation to use collaboration in order to break down its capacity to launch strategic initiatives. Each opportunity is entrusted to a "social community" called a council, office, or working group, depending on its estimated potential turnover.

"Instead of launching one initiative per year, as we used to do, we shall soon be able to run 30 of them in parallel."

Bluff? Between late 2005 and late 2009, Cisco's stock market capitalization rose by more than 15% while the cumulative value of its 11 main competitors sank by 60%.

This transformation took place at the cost of losing a fifth of its managers, who were unable to adapt to collaborative working, and at the cost of some major adaptations to John Chambers' own management methods.

In another industry, we find another legendary brand: Lego. On the verge of bankruptcy a few years back, since 2004 Lego has bounced back under the leadership of Jørgen Vig Knudstorp, one-time McKinsey consultant.

He is basing the Danish brand's strategy on the concept of a community of users.

The "My LEGO Network" has more than a million members. Among them, for a year 40 "ambassadors" from 22 countries have been directly involved in product development.

The Lego Factory program operates more widely, allowing each customer to create and order their own toys online and to join a community of creators. If an idea interests more than a thousand other people, the innovator receives 1% of the profits generated by their idea.

In France, too, many businesses are already making extensive use of collaborative tools to improve their performance. Naturally, the first to come aboard were the market leaders of the IT and telecommunications sector.

With "IdClic," Orange made spectacular economic performance gains, put at hundreds of millions of euros, thanks to a Web 2.0 participative innovation tool. That tool enabled 28,000 employees to issue,

comment on, and improve 93,000 suggestions and then allowed communities of experts to evaluate, validate, and arrange for the implementation
of 7,500 projects.

In the case of telecommunications giant SFR, a social network tool
has been used to facilitate the creation of microcommunities built around
items of common interest, and also to identify skills that standard human
resource (HR) systems cannot detect. For example, an engineer who
reveals that at weekends he acts as the treasurer of a voluntary group is
identified as possessing a skill that is potentially useful to the corporation
but that is not yet being exploited.

Toward New Forms of Organization

Enterprise 2.0 marks the advent of a new form of organization.

It is a commonplace to say that, over the course of the past two decades, the economy has moved from the *industrial* age to the *information* age. The source of value added has migrated, schematically, from the
physical production of goods (less and less profitable and gradually being
relocated to low-cost countries) to the processing of masses of data.

In response to this change in the value chain, there has been a corresponding change in business structures (see Figure A): purely "vertical"
and hierarchical organizations are gradually giving way to *matrix-based*
structures within which the center of gravity is tending to shift from ter-
ritories (sometimes seen as "empires") to global functions.

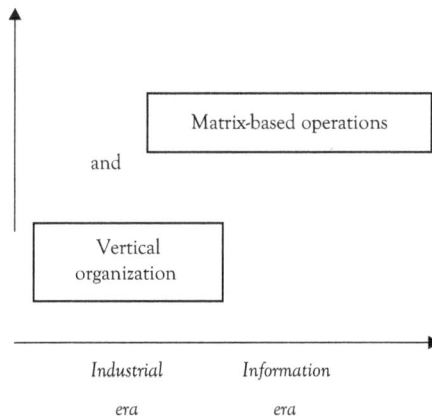

Figure A

Furthermore, the old pyramidal strongholds have seen their autonomy eroded by the remarkable upsurge in *project-based* institutions, which are of growing importance.

However, this form of organization is already being undermined by the shift from the *information* era to the *collaboration* era.

After the migration of manufacturing, it is the relocation of services that has begun on a significant scale. Occupations that involve the "mechanical" application of IT procedures are creating less and less value and are being exported to the emerging countries, which possess all the skills and resources required to perform those tasks, but with lower costs.

The creation of value is therefore more closely connected to the capacity of a corporation to innovate, to create, and to provide meaning, all functions that require intense and fruitful collaboration. That is the reason why *communities* are joining matrix and project-based organizations to build a new, more advanced form of organization (see Figure B).

Just as matrices and project teams did not eliminate vertical structures, communities are eliminating neither matrices nor project teams. They are complementing and enriching organizations.

Again, just as the center of gravity of organizations has tended to shift toward matrices and project-based structures, we can predict that it will continue to evolve and that one day communities will constitute the main dimension of corporations, whose community leaders could become their main leaders.

This trend is bound to have major consequences for leadership within organizations.

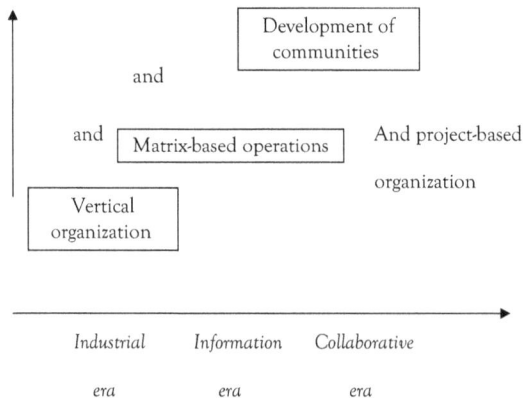

Figure B

When Social Learning Reinvents Training

A few years back, although numerous training methods already existed, skills development was essentially acquired through two conduits: attendance at courses and workplace support (tutoring, mentoring, work shadowing, sharing of good practice, etc.). Naturally, these two training methods still exist, but their relative importance is declining: *social learning* is growing apace.

We shall see how we now learn within a community, and shall then examine those Web 2.0 tools that are particularly well suited to skills development. Lastly, we shall examine the way in which training can create and inspire its own communities around strategic projects.

Learning Within a Community

In 2007, Danone, the global food manufacturer, began to organize events in a "marketplace" format.

At an annual convention bringing together some 200 people, the participants were given the option to explore a genuine farmer's market with authentic stalls, live chickens, and traders in costume.

Ten to twenty participants, who had been selected in advance for their skills, were the givers. They positioned themselves as vendors behind their stall in order to give an "elevator pitch" on the subject of a good practice whose effectiveness they had already been able to confirm.

The other participants, the "takers," were in possession of a chequebook allowing them to buy (on a virtual basis) those good practices that seemed best suited to their particular needs.

When they returned to their desks, the taker would get back in touch with the giver to discuss the good practice at greater length and in more detail.

The success of that marketplace won universal approval and it had a considerable impact on the corporation.

What should we call this Danone initiative?

It bears no relation either to a training course or to workplace learning within a typical team.

Without any technology at this stage, the marketplace is already allowing use to be made of "weak ties"[1] and it is even filling "structural holes" by allowing the participant to expand their network and exceed "Dunbar's number." It reinforces the feeling of belonging to a community, as defined by Mintzberg, and undoubtedly increases competence levels, fostering commitment, and a common culture.

This initiative is like many others, under which corporations train fast-track executives or geographically isolated people by making them work together within a community specially constructed for the occasion, on projects of common interest to the corporation.

For reasons of cost (travel costs, in particular) and administrative complexity, these operations have generally been reserved, until now, for very narrowly defined groups.

Web 2.0 tools overturn the old order by eliminating that obstacle.

Web 2.0 Tools at the Service of Training

In parallel with the marketplaces concept, Danone established an interactive tool designed for a test community.

Initially, a pilot project was developed with Danone Nature, a horizontal group comprising 250 people located around the world. This was so successful that the system was extended to cover every issue. At the time of writing, there are 200 active communities at Danone, involving employees based in 118 countries.

Employees learn from contact with colleagues facing the same challenges, but in different contexts. Not only are their skills developed, but they are more accurately identified: the tool effectively pinpoints isolated pockets of expertise. For example, the tool identifies an employee who has published 10 articles about vitamin D as an expert in this field, and their profile will come up when someone conducts a search concerning vitamin D. A new form of skills mapping is thereby emerging, providing managers and staff with greater transparency so that they know where they can find information and expertise.

There are many different social learning tools.

These days, blogs constitute a well-known means of accessing knowledge.

An expert publishes their discoveries, shares their analysis, gives their thoughts, and accepts the principle that other experts may provide further information in the comments section.

An employee can easily access the expert's most recent contributions and address new skills areas, use keywords to search for material on a topic of immediate personal interest, compare their views to those of the expert, and submit questions and comments.

Increasingly, uploaded videos constitute a highly prized form of expression. *Vlogs* or video blogs meet many users' expectations, whether they are experts or novices, better than text. For example, this is one of the most widely used tools at Cisco. Likewise, at Microsoft HQs in some countries, cabins are specially provided to allow any employee to record and upload a video clip.

Like vlogs, *podcasts* (audio/video files downloadable to a mobile terminal) are appropriate methods of accessing training. Useful knowledge can be accessed in a spare moment, or whilst traveling.

Forums give everyone a chance to put a specific question to a large number of people. Unlike mass emailing, which is often seen as intrusive and irritating, asking questions on a forum is widely accepted. What is more, as all responses are visible, each respondent can refine or add to responses already uploaded in order to provide the questioner with the most appropriate information.

Wikis allow you to produce collaborative documents, each person benefiting from the expertise of others in order to acquire a deeper understanding. The existence of a single document facilitates this process, compared to traditional methods that involve exchanging documents by email, which can easily cause frustration and lead to confusion. Similarly, the option to trace the items added by different contributors and, if necessary, to return to the previous version at any time makes the work even more efficient.

Lastly, rich site summary (popularly known as RSS) flows allow users to receive a brief alert whenever new content corresponding to personal areas of interest is uploaded. This can be in the form of a title, which also acts as a hypertext link allowing one-click access to the full content.

In short, in yesterday's world, an employee seeking specific information relating to their occupation generally had to either discuss with their boss or other immediate colleagues or wait to attend a training course in order to ask the trainer, with no certainty of obtaining an appropriate response.

In the world of today and tomorrow, thanks to social learning, upskilling is continuous, new material is frequently available, and answers to questions are almost immediate.

Creating and Organizing Training Communities Around Strategic Projects

Within large organizations, training is, more often than not, largely decentralized.

The people responsible for designing, leading, and administering projects and programs therefore need to be located as closely as possible to their internal customers.

Training managers and officers are scattered across the different regions of the world, and within each country across different business branches and within each business unit even across different occupations or roles: sales training is sometimes attached to the sales and marketing department or computer training to the information systems department.

Pendulum effects do exist: what was once decentralized will one day be centralized and vice versa, but unfortunately, in the meantime, pointless, energy-sapping power struggles and office politics often generate conflict between managers and operatives, between HQ and frontline, or between global and local structures.

For training work, it is not formal power that should be at stake. The true challenge is to be able to contribute effectively to the implementation of the strategy by developing skills, boosting commitment, and reinforcing a common culture.

That is why one of the priorities for the most advanced training departments is to establish communities that cross the organization's internal boundaries ... while recognizing and respecting them.

Whether or not they are hierarchically or functionally attached to a single central HR department, all the players involved in training must form a *training community*. This includes, for example, training representatives from small units who only perform this role on a part-time basis.

This *training community* comprises people who do not necessarily have the same priorities and are not always working on the same projects. However, they have points in common and all stand to gain from sharing experience and good practice, finding out about new project launches elsewhere and having the option to get advice from their peers.

Regardless of the training involved, these days any major strategic operation gives rise to the creation of one or more specific communities at head office level: whether the aim is to win customers, to innovate, to cut costs or to reorganize the company, it is unthinkable to implement a major initiative effectively without organizing a network of representatives active in every unit of the corporation.

John Kotter, Professor at Harvard and change management specialist, has long stressed the need to establish a *"guiding coalition"* for the successful deployment of a strategic initiative. He claims that this should be a group comprising *"people with a range of profiles, roles and levels of responsibility, but they should all be enthusiastic and ready and willing to roll up their sleeves to bring a project to life."*

For training, this means that, for each major program connected to the deployment of a strategic initiative, creating a *dedicated community* is an option that should be considered.

Apart from training providers involved in the project, this should include other key stakeholders: the senior executive sponsoring the initiative, managers responsible for operational delivery, local representatives for the strategic initiative (for whom training is one of the tools in their armory), external consultants, and trainers seconded to the project, etc.

The organization of communities, whether they are the trainers themselves or those receiving the training, therefore becomes the central focus for the training function.

More generally, as with any technological step change, the Web 2.0 revolution brings about profound change in organizations, patterns of behavior, and the rules of the game.

As with any revolution, this one is bound to cause a shake-up in many markets: not all corporations will be capable of taking maximum advantage quickly of these changes.

What does it take to be one of the winners?

A Successful Transition to Training 2.0

In 2009, McKinsey published an important study they carried out among corporations from every business sector and every part of the world that had deployed Web 2.0 tools.

More recently, in 2010, Korda & Partners teams began a wide-ranging benchmarking project on the establishment of 2.0 communities within corporations including Alcatel-Lucent, Capgemini, Danone, IBM, Microsoft, and SFR, among others.

The following recommendations are the fruit of lessons drawn from those two investigations and of direct experience of many Web 2.0 projects.

Overcoming Imaginary Problems

The introduction of social learning tools and 2.0 technologies, in general, is often greeted with serious misgivings.

Some of these relate to the potential behavior of employees.

Is there a danger that some employees will waste time in idle chatter, rather than concentrating on work? Is there not a risk that blogs and forums will be used to criticize the company or insult line managers? Will some online discussions cause controversy and needlessly generate a stressful atmosphere within the business?

On these issues, experience provides extensive evidence that self-regulation can work without major problems.

Certainly, collaborative tools can sometimes be used for discussions which have scant relevance to corporate objectives. Yet that is the case, too, with telephones (particularly mobiles) or gossip round the coffee machine. The only difference is that content posted on 2.0 tools remains on display, which can prevent nonwork topics getting out of hand.

Of course, some criticisms may be expressed, but these are generally moderate since they are not cloaked in anonymity. Such criticisms may also have the merit of alerting management to problems that are not being addressed and of reinforcing the general credibility of the tool: the online appearance of negative comments increases the credibility of positive opinions.

Naturally, some discussions may become heated, but generally speaking, *other* members of the community then intervene to ask those involved to abide by certain standards of behavior in form and substance.

Other misgivings concern the risk of the workforce being fed with inaccurate information. If anyone can use the tool to upload material, how can inappropriate content be identified?

Here again, experience shows that collective self-regulation allows erroneous uploads to be corrected very quickly, as we see with Wikipedia. Even if there is a need, in certain highly sensitive areas such as safety procedures, to check in advance content for uploading, this does not apply to the great majority of topics.

Lastly, other objections are associated with the risk inherent to the uploading of a mass of high-value information that could be diverted to the benefit of competitors.

Is it really worth taking the risk of putting in the public domain—and therefore open to unauthorized use—the accumulated expertise that the corporation has sometimes taken decades to build up?

This is the most serious objection as there is at present no reliable means of preventing the theft of information on a collaborative site.

However, the benefits of sharing knowledge clearly outweigh the disadvantages: for any corporation with access to collaborative tools, it is impossible to imagine forcing the workforce to go backward on the pretext of data protection.

Even an institution as sensitive to secrecy as the US Directorate of National Intelligence supported the creation of *Intellipedia*, a collaborative tool common to the sixteen agencies working on the prevention of terrorism, among other issues.

Doing Things in the Right Order: "Why?" Before "What?"

As our research proves, the vast majority of corporations that address the issue of social learning by looking at *tools* will fail. This is not for technical reasons, but because of the difficulties involved in getting a sufficient critical mass of users to take them up.

It is salutary to recall that even the greatest success stories on the web, like Wikipedia or YouTube, came about through the active participation of just a *tiny proportion* of the people with access to those tools.

If the same percentage is achieved within a corporation, it will mean that practically no-one will supply content and the project will be a complete failure.

In an article[4] in 2006, Professor John Gourville from Harvard demonstrated the existence of the "9x effect" when an innovation is introduced.

According to his research, people *introducing* an innovation tend to *overestimate* its benefits by a factor of 3. They are highly dissatisfied with the current situation, see an immediate need, and are convinced that the innovation will work, so they compare the preferred solution to other potential innovations.

In contrast, people who are *presented* with an innovation tend to *underestimate* its benefits to the same extent: they are generally satisfied with the current situation, skeptical about the predicted benefits, and compare the proposed innovation (which imposes immediate constraints on them, in exchange for an uncertain benefit at a later date) to the *status quo*.

Gourville claims that the innovation therefore needs to be at least nine times better than the existing solution to win people over. As quoted earlier, Andrew McAfee suggests that the failure of the "groupware" and "knowledge management" tools of the 1990s and 2000s was essentially due to the fact that they were then no more efficient than email.

Email has many benefits: it can be used very flexibly, can take a wide range of media (text, images, video, etc.), and requires no learning.

The fundamental issues to consider therefore concern, firstly, the desired objectives and the *anticipated benefits* of social learning tools, in the context of the implementation of the business strategy.

Does this require, for example, work on *strong ties* by encouraging more intense, training-oriented collaboration within a project team?

Is it better to concentrate on exploiting *weak ties* by giving employees the option to learn more within a much wider network, where relationships are more distant?

Is the aim to fill *structural holes* and to create connections between people who are currently completely disconnected?

In your situation, do the most useful functions involve the collective production of documents, the uploading of content (blogs, videos, podcasts, etc.) or the submission of questions to forums?

It is only after you have answered these "why?" questions that you will be able to examine the different options associated with the "what?": technologies, tools, functions, boundaries, etc.

Take care, though: our research indicates that in many cases, those who initiate projects tend to underestimate the social factor.

Finding a document is useful, but identifying its author is often even more so. Getting an answer is great, but knowing whom to put the next question to is even better.

This means that *social networking* is crucial.

Tackling the Real Enemy: Resistance to Change

Many corporations underestimate the difficulty of getting employees and managers to switch to a new generation of tools.

People will always respond differently to the collaborative web: some people create content, others merely comment, while others again will content themselves with reading that content … and others will be completely inactive. The proportions vary structurally from one type of group to another, but also depend on the way in which the project is managed.

To get people to switch, the first golden rule is to *embed new tools in your employees' everyday work.*

If an employee has to make a special effort to load up a software package to develop their skills without that tool being essential to their work, the software will generally remain unused.

It is therefore recommended to redesign certain processes to ensure that the 2.0 tool is "in the flow" and not "above the flow."

For example, a project manager may demand that any new contributions should be made via a wiki, to the exclusion of any other medium.

The management of a large business unit may cancel its newsletter in favor of a blog that will allow anyone to contribute to news production.

In certain circumstances, it may even be appropriate to ban all internal emails: employees can send personal confidential messages via the collaborative platform, but this allows them continuous access to the latter—and the opportunity to view new issues that are addressed there.

The second golden rule is to *have a "live" launch.*

A vibrant, lively community is never created by simply sending an email announcing that a collaborative tool has come online.

Business seminars and events often afford an opportunity to encourage support for 2.0 tools: participants see the community as a physical entity and the collaborative tools as something that will sustain it and help it to prosper.

Outside such meetings, on each site it is essential to be able to count on "missionaries" capable of stimulating, encouraging, and helping employees to use the new tools on an everyday basis.

Many representatives of "Generation Y" find it easy to play this role. They often feel completely at ease handling 2.0 tools and "evangelizing" to their more senior colleagues.

Lastly, the third golden rule relates to the *example set by management*.

It is important to show that top management believes in the tools. In Cisco's case, John Chambers himself now mainly uses vlogs to communicate.

Other senior managers prefer to write a personal blog, to comment on particular employees' blogs, or to put questions to the authors of wiki pages.

At the very least, the management needs to seize every opportunity to show that it uses the content generated by employees through collaborative tools. Quoting some information found in a blog or company forum during a convention or road show is a powerful method of boosting the esteem in which contributors are held.

To conclude this chapter, it is clear that the community dimension of corporations yields considerable training opportunities, especially but not solely in the context of strategy deployment.

Understanding the true nature of this community phenomenon and assimilating the characteristics of Web 2.0 are two essential preconditions, but this is not enough.

The real challenge lies in introducing social learning as a method that complements existing training methods by helping a wider range of employees from every group and generation to find their place in a new sort of business.

Without any doubt, this all requires a series of upheavals.

Fortunately, at this stage we can rely on a few certainties, starting with the need for small-group training and a certain conception of the role of the facilitator.

Sadly, however, the next chapter, entitled *Old Paradigms and New Formats*, suggests that even the best laid foundations may not be all they seem.

Key Points to Remember

- "Enterprise 2.0" could mark the advent of a new form of organization simultaneously composed of vertical lines, matrices, project-based structures, and communities, with a gradual shift in the power of influence from the former to the latter.
- In today's world, and in the future, thanks to social learning, upskilling is continuous, contributions are frequent, and answers to questions are almost immediate. Social learning is reinventing the way training is done.
  - Blogs now constitute a widespread means of accessing knowledge.
  - Online videos and vlogs, or video blogs, are better than text at meeting the expectations of many users, both experts and novices.
  - Podcasts, audio/video files downloadable to a mobile terminal, are an increasingly relevant means of accessing training.
  - Forums give everyone the chance to put a specific question to a large number of people.
- The organization of communities is becoming a central role of training providers.
  - communities of learners;
  - the training community;
  - communities devoted to the deployment of a strategic project.

Recommendations

The training connected to the implementation of our strategy ...	Yes!	More or less ...	Not yet
Does it use *weak ties* in order to allow everyone to learn from other colleagues whom they know but usually have little to do with?			
Does it fill "*structural holes*" by stimulating sharing between people from different units who were previously unaware of each other?			

(Continued)

(*Continued*)

Does it allow each employee to usefully expand their individual social network within the organization?			
Does it rely on *blogs* in which the corporation's experts share their knowledge and recent observations?			
Does it rely on *videos, vlogs, or both*?			
Does it give employees the option to access content via *podcasts*, for example, whilst traveling or during the odd spare moment?			
Does it give everyone the chance to put questions to a large number of people via a *forum*?			
Does it allow employees to produce documents collectively thanks to *wikis*?			
Is it taken forward by a *training community* involving all players and training providers, even if this is not their formal role?			
Is it taken forward by *dedicated communities* also involving sponsoring executives, middle managers, and external consultants?			
Do *head office blogs* feed into it?			
Is it spread through *head office comments on the blogs* of experts and other employees?			
Is its value increased by the fact that *head office refers to online content* in public?			

CHAPTER 6

Old Paradigms
and New Formats

What If the World Really Isn't Flat?

In 2010, a large European telecom operator sought to expand its production capacity, improve service quality and customer relations, and implement a new vision for human resources. It named its new strategic plan "Conquest."

The operations department, which employed 25,000 people including 2,000 middle managers, had a key role to play. Its 28 "support teams" were responsible for network construction and maintenance, including work on customers' premises, so they would be at the forefront of the drive to raise customer satisfaction.

Oliver, the company's Operations Director, had to ensure his staff were up to the challenge. Together with his teams, he designed and launched "New Support," an innovative professional vision based primarily on a culture of continuous improvement, customer responsiveness, and support for teams on the ground.

Implementing "New Support" was a major challenge. It required robust management structures to ensure that staff were able to adopt a new approach, work better collectively, and introduce lasting change quickly.

The company needed to train 2,000 middle managers with a technical background to make deep-seated changes in the way they worked. Those managers had already followed various management training programs in the past, so they would have to also be convinced that this new approach would obtain the desired results.

How could the corporation ensure that it achieved the changes required?

In this chapter, you will discover …

- *… that many training paradigms are now being swept away.*
- *… that the traditional 10-strong training group is on its way out when it comes to deploying a strategy.*
- *… that trainers as we have known them are also an endangered species, but that new roles and new occupations are springing up.*

The Rise and Fall of the Traditional Training Group

For years, all the airlines deemed it essential that each passenger boarding a plane should have a printed ticket comprising various flimsy detachable sheets.

The advent of electronic ticketing generated savings of tens of millions of pounds for the system and for customers, with no obvious problems to date.

Similarly, the training sector developed its own almost unanimously accepted principles, but these need to be reviewed. Many of them concern the size of training groups, the duration of training courses, and the presence of trainers.

The Group, a Key Element in Training! Or Is It …?

The need for a *group* is one of the rare points of consensus among educational specialists. "*You always learn alone, but never without others*," is a phrase often heard among teaching experts.

This conviction relies greatly on Kurt Lewin's discoveries in the postwar years.[1]

During food shortages, this remarkable American psychologist of German origin had tested various ways of training housewives to cook cheap cuts of beef, which were seen as less appetizing than the more noble parts of the animal.

The lectures given, successively, by an economist, a dietician, and a cook had won great plaudits. The individual lessons given to participants had also elicited great satisfaction. Unfortunately, in both cases, culinary habits had been unaffected: for 97% of those women, cheap cuts were served up no more frequently than they had been before they underwent training.

In practice, even if each participant had changed their personal perceptions of this issue, their opinions were not sufficiently firmly rooted to resist the combined weight of their personal habits and pressure from their family.

In contrast, a third method achieved greater success. This involved assembling small groups of mothers who were then asked, after lectures or personal tuition, for *recommendations* for the best way to *convince their peers* to cook cheap cuts of beef.

Those women did indeed forge a new opinion collectively that was much more robust and that determined their behavior as consumers despite their initial doubts.

This was all that was required for the idea of the *group* to be sanctified in the eyes of the educational experts: adults could only learn collectively.

The initial experiences of e-learning were marked by various setbacks, reinforcing this belief that the *group* was essential to training.

We are much less sure of that today.

For example, the continuous upsurge in *personal coaching* testifies to corporate interest in options that allow certain people to be given more in-depth support, particularly on a behavioral level. While this is a costly option that would be ill-suited to wide-scale use, it is clearly of growing importance.

The effectiveness of *online training* is now becoming crystal clear.

Taking the example of a major US government survey, comprising the "meta-analysis" of more than a 1,000 empirical studies carried out over 12 years, in 2009 this concluded that "*on average, students in online learning conditions performed better than those receiving face-to-face instruction.*"[2]

This means that there are situations in which individuals learn more effectively alone than in groups, particularly if the following three conditions are met.

Firstly, the person must be highly *motivated*, whether that motivation is *extrinsic* (e.g., the desire to earn a promotion or a qualification, or the fear of failing a test) or *intrinsic* (e.g., having a passion for the training topic or a firm desire to gain a better understanding of that issue in a work context).

Secondly, the individual must have access to *tools* allowing them to learn alone.

I am referring to cultural tools, like a good command of the language, basic computer literacy, and the ability to carry out research. Individuals from certain groups, who are used to working alone with IT tools, such as computer analysts or lawyers, are therefore better prepared than others.

I am also referring to the training tools themselves, which must suit the trainees' initial skills levels, in terms of the special expertise to be acquired but also that individual's learning style: as we saw in a previous chapter, a particular method can be a marvelous success with some people but a complete failure with others.

Lastly, of course, the training topic must be well suited to independent work, without the assistance of a group.

One area where this applies is the acquisition of specialist *knowledge*, but it also holds true for *coaching in individual tasks*, provided that this can give rise to automated feedback, without any human intervention. For example, certain operations are well suited, at least partially, to exercises on simulators that provide enough feedback to allow trainees to make progress on their own.

This means that the skills-development needs of certain individuals can be handled purely through self-tuition.

On the other hand, in many cases the group does fulfill indispensable functions.

As Kurt Lewin demonstrated, the group is a powerful motivational factor: it facilitates *awareness raising* and leads to more robust *changes in opinions* that encourage action, a crucial factor in situations of change.

Specialists in *group dynamics* have demonstrated the various consequences of discussions among small groups of people who have the opportunity to communicate among themselves.

In particular, although the phenomenon may be *imperceptible* to those people, a *pressure to conform* comes into play, meeting the needs of the individual for approval and certainty.

More specifically, imitative behavior occurs: each individual tends to adopt the same *standards of conduct* within the group, in order not to face "group sanctions" such as mockery. In addition, *emotional contagion* quickly sets in, together with the *emergence of collective values*: models, beliefs, legends, etc.

All these clearly constitute a potentially powerful lever to ensure training is effective in triggering the changes necessary to the implementation of a strategy.

The group also allows experiences to be shared among peers; more specifically, it affords opportunities for *social learning* (or *observational learning*).

This means that by watching another person complete a task successfully, an individual bypasses the usual process of learning by trial and error. They also often go beyond mere imitation: "*By extracting the rules underpinning the behavioral style of the model, people produce new models […] that go beyond what they have seen or heard. In addition, the modeling influences their motivation by instilling new and generally superior expectations regarding outcome.*"

We must note, though, that groups are not essential to social learning, which can also be achieved through workplace observation or by watching films, for example.

Lastly, a training group offers the corporation obvious practical benefits: a guarantee that all those employees required will complete the training according to the set schedule, "control" over behavior, handling of any doubts or objections, scale economies, etc.

In conclusion, contrary to deeply ingrained assumptions, while groups are often essential to training, this is *not always true* and *not necessarily at every stage*.

Ever more projects include some individual work and some group work, as we saw in the example of the engineering and construction business.

As regards the collective learning element, the question that follows naturally is: what is the optimum size for a training group? Once again, surprises are in store.

The Optimum Size for a Training Group: a Myth Debunked

Let us accept for a moment that it is useful to train staff members collectively, but what is the ideal number of people to bring together for a training course?

Many training specialists (working both within corporations and for specialist consultants) have a specific response.

It is often said that *eight* would be the ideal number. Any fewer and the discussions would not be fruitful enough, any more and the size of the group would inhibit the potential for all the participants to make an active contribution.

To take account of the need to cut the cost of the trainer for each group, other managers believe that *12* is a reasonable compromise between good management and the imperatives of efficiency. Some may even go as far as *14*, *15*, or even *18*, often by dint of increasing group size every year in order to adapt to increasingly tight budgets.

Then there are others who refine their analysis, believing that optimum group size varies according to the training topic. Thus, for training seminars addressing management, sales or interpersonal relations, *eight* people would be perfect. However, for subjects such as logistics or finance, *15* would do fine.

Apart from these nuances, the three widespread (and unchallenged) assumptions essentially state that: (a) There is an ideal group size, depending on the subject of the training; (b) That ideal size is a compromise between "too few" and "too many"; (c) Beyond that ideal size, any marginal increase would reduce the cost, and also the effectiveness of the training.

One logical consequence of this is that the idea of training people in very large groups is almost universally excluded, on the grounds that it would make it impossible for everyone to participate actively, to exchange questions and answers with the trainer, and to obtain personalized advice.

Yet certain corporations are now successfully challenging this approach, precisely where the training is directed at strategy deployment.

Their thinking is that ideal group size depends above all on the context of the business and the logic of the chosen means of deployment: by occupation, by region, etc.

Naturally, a retail chain, for example, will have to ensure that its sales outlets are continuously staffed: it will therefore generally be impossible to train every employee simultaneously.

It is also clear that a course attended by hundreds or even thousands of trainees will cause logistical problems that will usually be excessively complicated and costly to resolve.

Nevertheless, given their special constraints, these corporations are setting up training groups that are *as big as possible*: often comprising between 60 and 150 people.

In the strategy deployment context, training large groups does have several crucial advantages.

Firstly, it allows you to *considerably curtail the training schedule*: it is much quicker to train 10,000 people in groups of 150 than in groups of 12.

In itself, this accelerated deployment constitutes a crucial asset in achieving the changes anticipated.

When training programs extend over a long period and the employees from a single institution are trained at different times, implementation is tricky. We saw how postwar housewives[1] who left their training with a desire to cook cheap cuts of meat would often back down in response to disapproving looks from their families. Likewise, an employee who is prepared to change certain working habits will quickly throw in the towel if their closest colleagues continue to work as before.

That is why businesses use large groups to *train everyone immediately*. For example, Tesco in the UK was looking to train electronic and computer sale advisors in customer service which involved being available and approaching browsing customers on the shop floor to ask if they needed assistance. For the Tesco staff used to grocery retail the prevailing culture was to "look busy" and approaching customers was seen as "interfering." To shift the entire culture and provide the skills needed, they trained all the advisors in groups of 50–100 within 2 weeks.

Secondly, training large groups allows you to *get top management much more actively involved*.

When it comes to strategy deployment, the personal commitment of senior executives often makes all the difference. They mobilize line management, raise staff awareness of the objectives to be achieved, lend credibility to training programs, and boost the esteem of all those taking part in them.

Of course, it is impossible for the director of an institution employing 25,000 people, including 2,000 middle managers, to intervene personally in 200 training sessions each attended by 10 middle managers.

However, it enabled Oliver to participate in 20 sessions over a year, each attended by 100 middle managers. This allowed him to address each of them directly. That was the option chosen. The written feedback from the trainees reveals that the chance to meet the "top" boss and to ask him questions was a great stimulus for commitment, going beyond what had been imagined.

In the case of Adecco,[2] too, the active presence of senior operations managers at each of the sessions was crucial in mobilizing the sales and marketing managers.

Large-group training also allows staff members to *hear directly from the top internal and external experts.*

The personal impact of the trainer is crucial. Yet it is often just one or two people who have the skill, the charisma, and sometimes the prestige attached to past achievements enabling them to consistently win over all the troops.

Of course, for reasons of cost and availability it is physically impossible to bring these people to hundreds of sessions, whereas getting them to speak at a few large training events is feasible—and one fabulous trainer will have more impact in front of a 100 people than an average trainer will have in front of ten.

Lastly, if it is well run then large-group training allows you to fuel a *collective energy* quite out of proportion with the enthusiasm aroused by a training session involving 10–12 people.

In the case of our telecom operator, the participants' enthusiasm was visible—and audible: despite the difficult subject matter, those technically oriented middle managers used the theme of the "New Support" to compose some extremely entertaining songs and sketches. They forged a strong collective motivation that helped them to act individually as soon as they returned to the front line.

In the case of Adecco, this aspect was crucial to the success of the operation. It was on a wave of collective enthusiasm that, over the days following their seminars, the regional and area managers were able to disseminate the training sessions to their branch managers, to mobilize their teams, to overcome doubt, and to achieve the economic outcomes that are now familiar to us.

Naturally, the teaching methods used are very different from those traditionally employed.

For example, it is impossible to start a session with 150 people around a table taking turns to speak; but is that really such a bad thing? During traditional sessions, such round-table discussions take up precious time while adding little value: people generally pay little attention, just waiting for their turn, and wondering how to make a good impression. Other more productive and more efficient methods exist, both for "breaking the ice" and for allowing everyone to identify other group members.

In the case of our telecom operator, for example, they ask everyone multiple-choice questions. This starts with "survey" questions to discover the identity of the participants (*seniority, occupation, etc.*), then "opinion" questions to get course members thinking (*in your view, "New Support" is primarily about …?*). The approach is crisp, well paced, and interactive.

It is also impossible to put every participant in turn in front of the whole group for an exercise; but, even in a group of ten, is it really appropriate for each member to spend 90% of the exercise in a passive situation? It is more useful to allow all those taking part to train individually or in pairs on tightly defined objectives, as we saw in Chapter 2.

It is obviously impossible to properly debate the trainer's input with the entire group; but is that a disadvantage, when we know that, even in a small group one or two participants generally monopolize 85% of the speaking time?

It is also impossible for the participants to raise detailed issues or specific cases with the trainer every other minute. That said, in traditional sessions, just how much time do participants waste listening to questions and answers about subjects that they already understand—or that do not concern them? Furthermore, the Web 2.0 technologies discussed in Chapter 5 now let them pose questions and obtain clear answers from an expert or other competent individuals and access the answers given in any other session, without needing to spend more than a few moments on this.

It is still generally essential for each participant to be able to benefit personally from expert guidance.

That is why large-group sessions almost always include a sequence during which the participants work in *very small groups* with the support of an internal or external consultant.

In the case of Tesco, they worked in smaller groups to practice soft selling skills and building confidence to approach customers receiving constructive criticism of a Korda & Partners coaching consultant, an executive board member, and several other middle managers.

Likewise, when the Onet Cleaning and Multiservices division trained all its sales representatives to promote the excellence of its services to customers, it organized a *launch* session in each region, followed by *coaching* sessions, and a *closing* session.

The launch and closing sessions brought together about 30 people: the regional director and his assistant, plus all the branch managers, sales representatives, and operations managers for that region. In contrast, the coaching sessions were held in tiny groups of just six people, with a coaching consultant.

Lastly, it is clear that large-group training sessions can only prove effective if the participants are continuously *active*.

Too often, large-group seminars inflict long sessions comprising hundreds of slides, personal accounts, round-table discussions, videos, and theatrical performances on a completely passive audience.

Yet it is perfectly possible to employ appropriate methods to generate as much participation from a group of 150 people as from a group of 10. That participation simply has to take different forms: a show of hands in response to questioning by the group leader, the use of audience response systems to vote on multiple-choice questions, short sequences focusing individually on an ongoing situation, exercises to be completed in pairs, practical tasks to be done in teams, etc.

In conclusion, the myth that you can only train people properly in groups of ten has lasted long enough: when it comes to deploying a strategy, the most advanced corporations are increasingly likely to opt for training in very large groups, using specially adapted teaching methods, supplemented by coaching sessions or in-depth work carried out in very small groups.

Three Days Together in a Single Room: "That Was in the Old Days!"

Apart from the issue of group size, the question arises as to the duration of the training and the ways in which people are brought together.

With regard to management issues, for example, it had long been seen as impossible for training work to be sufficiently thorough to yield results unless it lasted for at least three to four consecutive days.

As everyone knows, for years many corporations have been seeking to cut the duration of training courses and such long sessions are on their way out.

As we saw in a previous chapter, people are noticing the benefits of breaking training up into a series of short sessions interspersed with implementation phases.

However, in practice, this more fragmented approach does pose various problems. In particular, in the case of personnel who are widely dispersed geographically, it increases staff travel, and the associated time and costs.

These days, when corporations opt for group training, which is no longer always the case, they sometimes experiment with other formats, often successfully.

Firstly, they seek to *start training before the course.*

In particular, employees are encouraged to acquire the *knowledge* essential to the training before they attend the group sessions, generally through e-learning modules.

Many of the corporations already cited throughout this book apply that method.

Sometimes employees even have to *do some operational work in advance*, which will then be used during the training session.

For example, after they have benefited from four e-learning modules, TF1 middle managers are invited to produce a "road map" with their team according to a specific method laid down for them in a practical guide, before they participate in the seminars that are on offer.

According to a study conducted in March 2010, 42% of European employees have already experienced e-learning, while 54% of employees in Spain have already benefited from training of this type.

In other cases, employees are also asked to specify their needs and expectations, to select particular cases that they would like to tackle during the training course and, sometimes, to prepare some preparatory diagnostic work on those cases.

All these approaches are designed to refocus the "face-to-face" session on specific value-added features: discussion, coaching, feedback, and collective motivation.

Secondly, these corporations are experimenting with ultrashort formats: now referred to as *small-dose training.*

Such methods have existed for a long time, but only in certain restricted fields: it is no surprise to anyone if a colleague is away for 2 hours attending a language class or a coaching session. Yet commercial or managerial training courses are not generally designed to take place over such a short timescale.

This is in the process of changing, particularly thanks to new, quicker, high-impact teaching methods, some of which we have already described.

For practical reasons, this "small-dose training" is staged either directly in the workplace (especially for head office staff) or at specially prearranged events: executive conventions, monthly departmental meetings, etc.

This may involve training programs that are absolutely crucial to the deployment of a strategy. Thus, when SPIE Matthew Hall wanted to implement a new strategic focus on "environmental energy" in the UK, they developed short "toolbox" sessions delivered by managers to all employees within 1 month.

Lastly, recent advances in communications technology are allowing corporations to organize *virtual training classes*, thereby eliminating distance and travel costs.

This process is certainly no innovation. The American group health insurance giant Aetna Life was already using virtual classes to train employees scattered across several time zones back in 1995. At that time, it was quite some technical feat.

These days, "off-the-shelf" tools have become widespread and accessible, bandwidths have expanded, and most work stations can easily support the applications required.

In Spain, 30% of employees have already benefited from access to such training.

Meanwhile, throughout Europe, corporations such as the Xerox Group have successfully rolled out virtual training classes for their sales representatives. Xerox's classes form part of a comprehensive system that also encompasses face-to-face sessions and e-learning modules.

The software used at Xerox allows all participants to benefit from training merely by connecting to the internet. The interface comprises three screens, each of which has a quite specific purpose: the first is devoted to organization, the second allows you to see the group, while the third allows each participant to pose questions at any time.

Apart from the highly "image-oriented" talks from the facilitator, the learning includes case resolution, multiple-choice exercises, and knowledge tests in the form of games, which make the sessions interesting and interactive.

More generally, training is taking on a "multichannel" format. In banking or mass retailing, the consumer has several means of accessing the distributor. These can be used to the optimum to suit personal preferences and needs. The training of the present and the future combines different methods of accessing skills, which are placed at the disposal of the workforce.

We can therefore see that, when it comes to deploying a strategy, the traditionally long seminar attended by a group of ten people is losing ground on a massive scale, due to the development of self-tuition via e-learning, in training both large groups and very restricted groups, the advent of shorter, more segmented and better-prepared formats, the perfection of virtual classes, etc.

We may be sure that all these raise serious doubts over the role of the trainer.

Do We Still Need Trainers?

For years, books have been published about the role of the trainer, whether employed in-house or by a specialist institution.

Many of those books, often of excellent quality, have placed particular emphasis on three basic skills.

First and foremost, if not an expert a good trainer should at least have a good knowledge of the issues that they are addressing. They will possess expertise and the participants will seek to acquire some of this. It has been the information and experience at the trainer's disposal that make them valuable.

The trainer should also be an excellent *popularizer*. Their explanations should be accessible to all, and illustrated by simple examples and stories that stick easily in the mind.

Lastly, they should be an *independent facilitator*, able to work alone so as to handle group discussions without being swamped, to ensure that everyone present participates and to keep everyone's attention throughout the training sessions.

Naturally, these qualities are still useful.

However, in the context of the deployment of a strategic initiative, the consistency of the message is so important that corporations try to define it as tightly as possible; there is no question of allowing the message to vary depending on the session or the group leader.

The format of the training content is therefore often so precisely defined by the different teaching media that the trainer has little opportunity to use their special knowledge.

In addition, in a world where almost everyone is online, *knowledge* is now freely available; it no longer defines the value of the person who has it. Information is accessible, already *popularized* through different sources and in different forms. An employee seeking information no longer waits to meet a trainer in order to ask a question: by the time they arrive at the course, they have already found the answer in an e-learning module, on a community network, or simply by browsing the internet.

The group leader is certainly bound to know more than the trainee.

However, what counts is that the trainer should know how to motivate and to help staff members to apply the skills required in practice.

For example, at IKEA certain training programs in point-of-sale work take place in a room located on the site of a shop. The leader then shares their personal front-line experience and once a sequence has been completed, the participants enter the sales area and immediately put what they have learned into practice.

In addition, with strategy implementation, which is highly outcome dependent, the quality of the *leadership* in the training room is ultimately a *basic expectation*; it is a minimum requirement, but not enough to satisfy those in charge.

In practice, without the effective involvement of staff trainers in implementation, training will generally have little impact.

If they want to survive the ongoing revolution, trainers must therefore make two fundamental changes: they must become *operations coaches* and *managers' partners*.

When the Trainer Becomes an Operations Coach

To help employees to put the requisite skills into practice, the trainer is increasingly required to work with "*natural teams*."

Within many businesses, training sessions do bring together people from different institutions.

For the training department, this format has the advantage of facilitating planning and ensuring full course take-up. Most importantly, it helps each participant to expand their social network within the business and thereby contributes, albeit only marginally, to the much-trumpeted ambition of "decompartmentalization."

If implementation principally relies on strictly individual actions, these "interinstitutional" sessions do not pose any major problem.

Where it is vitally important to the strategy to ensure better cooperation between institutions, it can even be indispensable, as in the case of TF1.

On the other hand, in many cases, a strategy will mainly be adapted to suit each basic unit of the business.

This means that there are enormous benefits to *training the whole team together, manager included*: the opportunity to address team-specific obstacles to implementation, the development of an action plan, the allocation of roles, the manager's supervisory arrangements, etc.

In the case of Onet cleaning and services business in Europe, it was within each regional department that the project was implemented. At Adecco, it was within the national customers department and each operations unit, and then each region and area that the training project was rolled out.

For trainers, the situation is not at all the same.

When faced with a group of employees from different units, they are in a position of strength to some extent.

At the start of the session, each participant is slightly nervous of the others. This means that it is quite easy for a good leader to exert influence over the group.

For example, the trainer can put the group members on the back foot with a few questions or exercises. They can also demonstrate the extent of their knowledge by putting on a good "show": figures, dates, anecdotes, quotations, specific examples, photos, videos, special effects, etc. Lastly, they can win the group over by appealing to the personal characteristics of each individual in attendance.

When the group raises specific cases, these can often only be tackled quite superficially, given the number of different situations represented in the room. Furthermore, group members do not generally have the decision-making powers necessary to tackle those cases when they return to the workplace: this means that there is little at stake in training room discussions, so the trainer can put on a dazzling, but risk-free performance.

When faced with a proper working team, the balance of power is quite different.

The group members will know one another well and will quickly share their impressions of the leader.

In addition, given the factors involved in group dynamics, there is a strong and spontaneous resistance to new ideas. Any changes rendered necessary by the implementation of the strategy will not necessarily be readily accepted. Any intervention by the trainer that is seen as critical of a participant may also encourage a closing of the ranks and a harsh collective response.

Most importantly, the employees and their line managers will often arrive with firm and specific collective expectations. Thus, when a specific case is raised, a decision will need to be taken and its effectiveness may be tested in practice.

For the trainer, the key skill is no longer therefore *the ability to transmit knowledge, but to help ensure that it is properly applied, contributing to the implementation of the strategy.*

The trainer *represents the strategic project vis-à-vis the participants.* This assumes that they have fully understood its challenges, objectives, and different dimensions.

Some *practical* experience is also essential, whether this has been acquired through operational responsibilities or, potentially, in various supporting roles.

This experience helps to give the trainer the *legitimacy* necessary to deal with natural teams.

However, having skills similar to those of other individuals is insufficient to allow you to train them properly.

Aside from their charisma and the essential ability to motivate others, a trainer must simultaneously possess *explicit* knowledge, *tacit* expertise, an *observant* nature, and the ability to *probe.*

Imagine having to perform brain surgery after you have read every published book on the subject. Those books will give you all the *explicit* knowledge that is available, but performing a successful operation requires other forms of *tacit* knowledge, which are only acquired through observation, gradual participation, and the experience of carrying out that task. A trainer needs both dimensions of knowledge—the explicit and the tacit.

Observation is what allows the trainer to look beyond a case raised by group members to discern *how they perceive, address, and handle that case*, which by definition constitutes part of the problem.

Probing is what distinguishes a "coach" from a mere lecturer.

A trainer cannot be expected, on their own, to find the solutions to all those problems that teams have been unable to cope with until then. However, through probing questions, the trainer can guide those employees toward ways of thinking and acting that they would not have explored of their own volition.

Thus, the trainers of the present and the future will be able to work with natural teams, to tackle specific cases with a group, but also to lend *support toward implementation* in various ways, such as telephone follow-up or workplace support.

For example, on day two of the "New Support Campus" sessions, in-house trainers led small-group workshops.

Pretrained by external consultants, they helped the middle managers to put the improvement loop principles into practice immediately in a realistic working scenario.

As we can see, the traditional trainer is giving way in favor of the operations coach.

But can that coach work alone?

When the Manager Becomes the Initial Trainer

It is commonplace to hear that "the manager must pass the training on to their staff."

Yet this is not always true: for some purely technical training programs meeting an employee's specific working needs, the immediate line manager adds little value.

Furthermore, surveys reveal that in Europe managers only cascade training in 13% of cases. Even the top-performing UK only achieves a figure of 31%.

Nevertheless, when training is meant to facilitate the deployment of a strategy, the role of the line manager far surpasses that of a mere "messenger."

With increasing frequency, the line manager is called upon to produce the "road map" adapting the strategy to the area for which they are responsible and then to play an active role in training up their team.

This role breaks down into five elements.

The manager plays an active part in *diagnosing the training needs* of their staff.

As we have already seen, this does not only merely involve identifying the weaknesses of particular individuals in the relevant area, but also conducting analysis on three levels: the specific skills necessary for strategy deployment, the individual and collective degree of mastery of each of those skills (unknown, weakness, strength, and culture), and the training approaches likely to generate the quickest and most productive progress.

Secondly, the manager makes each staff member *aware* of the importance of the training.

This is often achieved through a formal interview during which the manager and employee discuss the impact of the strategy on the employee's work, operational challenges to be addressed, particular difficulties where training may be of assistance, specific circumstances to be dealt with, and follow-up work to be carried out immediately after training.

For the manager, this also involves encouraging each staff member to use the self-tuition tools available and to prepare carefully for each of their sessions.

It is also ever more common for the manager to *take responsibility for some of the training*.

For some commercial networks, such as chains of pharmaceutical laboratories, running training sessions has long been part of the job description for supervisors.

However, apart from such cases, it is not always straightforward to entrust all middle managers with a role in classroom training.

Indeed, a single session rarely offers enough preparation time to fully assimilate a training module. Benefits therefore do not accrue either in the form of scale economies or a learning curve.

There is also a serious risk that the training may not be enough to yield an optimum impact for the whole workforce: whether because, in certain cases, the manager has not taken the time to prepare properly, or, in others, they do not possess the personal skills required to be a good trainer,[3] or they sometimes lack sufficient personal *credibility* to handle the subject of the training, given their behavior or usual practices in the area concerned.

That is why, although he or she may be the initial trainer, the manager generally only takes responsibility for part of the training.

At PricewaterhouseCoopers, the Consulting Academy is a training system that allows them to implement their management consultancy strategy.

All sessions intended for senior and middle managers in this field are jointly run by a Consulting Partner with a specialist trainer. The Partner helps to connect all the trainer's input to the corporation's policy, uses real-life examples to reinforce the main messages, and helps to run the exercises that are staged.

In other cases, training sessions are initially organized by a trainer, and then by a manager who administers this small-dose booster training at their regular team meetings. This involves offering their personnel a short series of refresher sessions and practical coaching, based on centrally designed tools.

Lastly, the middle manager reinforces the impact of the training through *operational coaching initiatives*, which complement those run by the trainers.

This might involve observing a colleague at work and then helping them to identify ways of further boosting their performance, or playing the role of a sparring partner to help a team member to prepare for an important meeting with a customer or partner.

Not all these training roles adopted by the manager are new, but they certainly constitute a growth area.

Having become the initial trainer of his or her teams, the middle manager is no longer a mere "evaluator," but also a coach keen to exploit the potential of each individual in order to maximize performance levels and implement the strategy.

Naturally, this development itself has a strategic aspect, and line managers are trained to take on this new role. Thus, a *coaching stance* is highly valued under various recent programs for middle managers at L'Oréal.

In conclusion, training has clearly changed a great deal!

In the past, it was led by a trainer with a group of about 10 trainees, but now it takes many forms: self-tuition, very large and very small groups, coaching, virtual classes, workplace support, community-based web sites, etc.

Trainers will become operations coaches and will successfully share their role with middle managers or they will gradually become extinct.

The scale of the needs is immense. For a long time, training was a stable world within which methods changed only very slowly, like teaching methods in schools. There have been enormous changes—and they have probably only just begun.

The five previous chapters allowed us to focus on the *way* of using training in order to deploy a strategy effectively.

The next chapter, entitled *The Quest for Return on Investment*, addresses the leadership of this activity from both an economic and a strategic perspective.

Key Points to Remember

- While groups are often indispensable to training, this is not always so—and not at every stage.
- An individual can learn in isolation if they are highly motivated, they possess the resources, and tools needed for autonomous learning and the training topic lends itself to this.
- However, in many cases, a group offers important advantages: motivation, opportunities for *social learning*, practical, and economic benefits.
- In the context of the deployment of a strategic initiative, training *large groups* allows you to
  - curtail the training schedule,
  - get top management involved,
  - mobilize the top experts,
  - generate collective enthusiasm that is beneficial to implementation.

- These large-group sessions must be organized using teaching methods that ensure the participant is very active, complemented by working sessions in *very small groups.*
- Long training sessions are tending to disappear.
  - Training programs are broken up into a series of short sessions interspersed with phases of practical implementation.
  - Businesses seek to ensure that "training starts before the course."
  - They are experimenting with ultrashort formats: small-dose training.
  - They are organizing training programs through virtual classes.
- Trainers are becoming operations coaches.
  - They are dealing ever more with natural teams, with the manager included.
  - They represent the strategic project, so they are fully cognizant of its challenges, objectives, and different dimensions.
  - They are able to provide individual support toward implementation by telephone or in the workplace.
  - They have a simultaneous mastery of explicit knowledge, tacit expertise, the ability to observe, and the art of probing.

Recommendations

The training connected to the implementation of our strategy	Yes!	More or less	Not yet
Does it use *self-tuition* whenever the conditions for success are met?			
Does it follow the logic of optimum deployment: for example, by occupation or region?			
Does it allow you to *train everyone immediately?*			
Does it at least allow *all staff members from a particular unit* to be trained more or less simultaneously?			

(Continued)

(*Continued*)

Does it alternate *very large-group* and *very small-group* sessions?			
Does it get *top managers personally involved* in all sessions?			
Does it offer all staff the opportunity to *listen directly to the top experts* on the subject?			
Does it generate a powerful wave of *collective enthusiasm*?			
Does it ensure that the participant is *active from start to finish* of sessions, even in very large groups?			
Is it *broken up* into a series of short sessions interspersed with phases of practical implementation?			
Does it begin *before the first session* with self-tuition through e-learning, individual operational work, and the preparation of case studies to be tackled during the training course?			
Does it include small-dose training, ultrashort sessions organized either directly in the workplace or at prearranged events?			
Does it include sessions in *virtual classes* for geographically dispersed populations?			
Does it address *natural teams (manager included)* whenever implementation principally takes place at the level of the unit?			
Is it entrusted to trainers able to *represent the strategic project* vis-à-vis staff members and managers?			
Is it entrusted to trainers endowed with *sufficient front-line experience*?			
Is it entrusted to trainers endowed with a real capacity *for observing* the way in which staff address problems?			
Is it entrusted to trainers endowed with a real capacity *for probing* to get employees to find the solutions themselves?			
Is it entrusted to trainers able to provide *support toward implementation* by telephone or in the workplace?			

Does it make *line managers* the initial trainers?			
Does it get line managers to *analyze their teams' specific needs*?			
Does it get line managers to make each staff member *aware* of the importance of their training?			
Does it give line managers an active role in *leading* or *jointly leading* sessions?			
Does it give line managers an active role in the *operational coaching* of their staff?			
Does it give *trainers and line managers* complementary and well-defined roles?			

CHAPTER 7

The Quest for Return on Investment

Training Doesn't Have to Be a Cost!

A global electrical engineering group which employs more than 100,000 staff across a hundred countries and has a turnover of almost $16bn, positions itself as a global specialist in *energy management*.

Its activities range from initial energy production through to energy use and ensuring that the energy supplied is safe, reliable, productive, and "green."

While the issue of energy production is crucial, *energy management* is just as important: it is currently estimated that the global demand for energy will double by 2050 and that 70% of that increase will come from the emerging countries. The stakes are high for the economy but even more so for the environment and the climate.

To support its strategy and to meet market expectations as effectively as possible, the company is undergoing a revolution. The group is transforming itself from a products manufacturer into a supplier of integrated and customized solutions capable of servicing its customers' specific needs to the highest possible standards while increasing its presence in emerging markets.

Training is carried out by teams spread across Europe, the Americas, and Asia. More than 200 people are responsible for designing and managing its skills-development programs. The production of training programs and tools is largely outsourced to other organizations. This requires large-scale resourcing.

How can the corporation ensure that those resources really are used effectively to promote its strategy? How can it accurately gauge their impact? How can it improve their cost/efficiency ratio?

In this chapter, you will discover ...

- *... that you are not the only one wondering whether you are really asking the right questions, and, on a strategic level, how you are using your training resources;*
- *... that the most fashionable evaluation methods are not necessarily the most appropriate;*
- *... the economic savings that are within your grasp thanks to "cost-effective training".*

Strategic Training Seen From Outside

Training work is characterized by a constant need to switch between the general and the specific, between the short term and the long term.

For such work it is essential to understand an organization's strategic challenges and the impact these have on professions and jobs, and to identify quite disparate individual and collective needs, while continuing to manage various short-term and often urgent projects.

That is why it is sometimes difficult to retain the distance necessary to identify your true priorities.

What are the truly essential questions to ask if your training is to promote your strategy effectively? We shall endeavor to respond firstly at company level and then at project level.

At Company Level

For the late lamented Peter F. Drucker, "Management is about doing things right; leadership is about doing the right things."[1]

Indeed, the first question to ask from a strategic perspective is "Does our training address the right subjects?"

When the Group Learning & Development Director took up his global responsibilities, he wanted to be clear in his own mind.

Firstly, he assessed the corporation's strategic priorities and their implications for human resources (HR), and then he analyzed the degree to which its training met each identified need.

Secondly, from the ongoing training projects in different continents and the resources allocated to training, he calculated the proportion used for work that really was connected to strategic priorities. He also distinguished customized programs from basic "off-the-shelf training courses."

Lastly, he asked the senior managers of the group's business units (its internal customers) what they expected of training: what training activities did they see as the most crucial? He then consolidated and analyzed the timesheets of the various team managers to identify those activities to which the training managers were actually devoting their energies.

He made a fascinating—and startling—discovery.

For the most part, the corporation's strategic priorities correlated perfectly with global or local training projects. However, the alignment was still not perfect.

In some countries, just 40% of all training resources were allocated to strategic priorities. When the customized programs are viewed in isolation, those best suited to meeting the challenges of the group or its institutions, that 40% figure falls as low as 20%.

Three main activities help to align training with strategy: firstly, responsiveness to internal customers and "business" needs, via a "performance-consulting" approach; secondly, having a single coordinator for all an institution's projects; and, lastly, the systematic measurement of project efficiency or return on investment (ROI).

Yet these three activities together accounted for less than 40% of training managers' working time.

The team comprised excellent professionals who used the revelation of this data to reassess their activities and to rapidly refocus on their true priorities.

At a company level, strategic training management requires you to ask yourself questions of three kinds.

The first kind relates to the *training needs associated with your strategy*.

Everything starts with an inventory of the activities affected by your main priorities and strategic projects, at the level both of the group and its main divisions.

This does not merely involve identifying the *changes* needed but also, more generally, the *new* activities to be introduced, the *weaknesses* to be remedied, the *strengths* to be reinforced and the areas in which you already have a strong *business culture* but where your strategy requires you to constantly quest after *excellence*.

You then need to identify the groups concerned. Some employees do *jobs* that are crucial to the implementation of a strategy. *Senior executives* and *middle managers* always have a key role to play. More and more frequently, consideration also has to be given to *customers*; it may also be essential to train them, when products and services change quicker than the habits of the market.

Naturally, demographic data should be taken into account in assessing the scale of the needs ... you need to examine anticipated changes in the workforce and the number of people expected to arrive or depart.

This initial analytical phase allows you to define your training objectives and to position your main projects.

The second series of questions concerns the *allocation of the financial resources for training*.

What proportion of those resources should be allocated to training initiatives directly connected to strategic priorities?

From among those resources, what proportion should be devoted to general programs, as opposed to local projects, or to horizontal initiatives as opposed to measures addressing particular occupations?

What proportion should be devoted to special training for line management as opposed to the general workforce?

Logically, to what extent should you focus on customized programs as opposed to packages selected from a catalog?

The answers will depend on the company's specific context. However, in most cases, as we saw with the global engineering company above, a comparison with the current distribution of resources reveals immediate opportunities for adjustment.

A third series of questions relates to the strategic use of *HR in training*.

Of course, there are personnel working for training departments.

In training terms, is their distribution by country, company role, hierarchical level, and specialist expertise appropriate to the development of your strategic challenges?

Are you making the right spending decisions on the training design and management work that is outsourced and the work entrusted to trainers in-house?

In-house trainers usually offer the advantage of ensuring that training programs are fully consistent with the business culture. In the case of recurrent mass training programs, they can also cost less per day than the fees charged by external organizations.

This resource is well suited, then, to firms operating in stable environments that are endowed with great expertise that they can share and exploit.

In contrast, external trainers can provide higher value-added to support change, benchmarking, and innovation. In situations of change, they also enjoy greater credibility in the eyes of your staff because of their experience of other firms and business sectors. They also represent a flexible cost and can easily be made to compete with others.

This means that external consultants are well suited to situations of change.

Lastly, are you taking full advantage of *middle managers'* skills and their presence within their teams to bolster your training?

When the stakes are at their highest, what is required is the best possible combination of these three types of resources (in-house trainers, external consultants, and line management).

At Project Level

At the above-mentioned global electrical engineering firm, the training engineering managers are genuine in-house consultants trained to address the "root causes" of any performance shortcomings discovered and to use standard strategic analysis and project management tools and methods to tackle each major issue.

Seen from the outside, each major training project raises different types of issues.

The first concerns the *objectives* of the project: it is essential to fully understand the strategic ambitions that the training is designed to promote, and then to define precise and realistic outcomes expected of that training, before evaluating the economic implications.

The economic implications will largely determine the resources to be allocated to that operation.

Here is an example of ten key questions on the objectives of a major training project.

1. What *strategic ambition* is the training going to serve and what are its various dimensions and implications?

2. What are the specific *initiatives*, the *ways of working* and, more generally, the *behavior* expected to help achieve that strategic ambition?

3. Which are the particular *categories of people* most likely to put such behavior *into practice* and in which *work situations* will they be specifically obliged to demonstrate this?

4. What is the *disparity* between the current situation and the situation expected?

5. Within what *timescale* is that disparity to be reduced?

6. Is it *realistic* to expect those people to behave like that in those work situations and within that timescale? What examples and other evidence can convince you of this?

7. If we assume that this behavior manifests itself and becomes more widespread through training, what will be the *visible and measurable results?*

8. Are those results *credible*? Is there a proven causal connection between the behavior and the results?

9. In general, what are *the economic implications* of the operation?

10. Taken overall, which *indicators* shall we use to determine whether the training project has been a success in relation to the strategy?[1]

The second series of questions relates to the *conditions for success*.

There is a need to identify the enablers and challenges of every kind that may significantly impact the success of the operation.

Firstly, the question arises as to the *meaning* given to the project. Will staff members benefit from clear information justifying the strategy and its consequences for their own work? Has the firm's message been delivered, heard, understood, and accepted? Is it generating anxiety, enthusiasm or indifference?

This issue of *meaning* is closely connected to that of *alignment*: Are the various priorities that the organization has assigned to an individual coherent or are they contradictory? Are the personal evaluation and performance-measurement indicators and systems (and potentially even performance-related pay) consistent with the strategy and with the conduct expected or are they at odds with one another?

Then, among the preconditions for success, comes the issue of other people: apart from those groups most directly affected, in all probability *other groups of people* are likely to help or to hinder the achievement of the behavior expected.

Among the latter, senior management is clearly the first concern.

Obviously, *immediate line management* is also a priority: training line management before their staff and involving them in project implementation is an imperative that brooks no exception.

In the case of long line management chains, each level must be tackled specifically and successively. It is crucial that each tier should feel that is being given some responsibility vis-à-vis its own staff.

It is certainly tempting to group all supervisory staff together, perhaps within a region, for a condensed form of training. Yet such initiatives may induce apathy in the most senior management tier attending that meeting if those managers feel that they are being "denied" their due responsibilities.

Thus, where a general meeting of supervisory staff seems to be the best solution (e.g., to take advantage of a meeting that has already been scheduled), you should at least prepare for the event with executive management. Then specifically with senior managers, in order to involve them in the shared challenge and finally focusing on encouraging commitment from first line management.

As well as supervisory staff, another crucial category of people involved in strategic training projects is *local management*, executives sometimes discussed in disparaging terms at head office.

These are the managers who work at some distance from headquarters, either quite literally, due to geography, or simply because they are appointed to perform work other than the corporation's main business activity.

They are often dynamic middle managers with a great ability to take the initiative, but also strong on personality. By necessity and then by habit, they have sometimes gradually strayed from or even taken a few liberties with general management instructions.

Thus, major head office initiatives generally receive a grudging response from these local managers.

This is particularly true for strategic training projects. There will be no shortage of objections. The standard objections include "*That might work fine in London, but it doesn't meet our priorities here,*" "*the content doesn't suit the culture of our organization," "We've been doing all that for ages here, so we'd be wasting our time on this training," "We've not got that far yet here and our staff won't understand this training at all,"* etc.

This raises the issue of the relevance of large, homogenous training programs to the deployment of a strategic priority at the *group* level.

For corporations endowed with a very strong culture of their own, like many American multinationals, this issue does not arise: major training initiatives are rolled out within such corporations *worldwide on a strictly identical basis* and help to further reinforce the culture of that organization.

In the case of more disparate organizations, including those created through a series of recent mergers and acquisitions, a choice must be made between immediate efficiency (an argument for significant adaptation to local circumstances) and the desire to integrate.

A study carried out in 2008, encompassing 20 multinational companies, revealed that several approaches coexist in such circumstances.

Certain corporations opt to pursue training projects on a general basis, with the support of consultants who are responsible for their design and universal implementation.

This is the case at the electrical engineering company, where a "Group Leadership Academy" brings together all its development services worldwide, catering to the group's 14,000 middle managers.

It is also the case, for example, with some of those training programs at a global IT giant that are the most directly connected to a "Top Operational Performance" program.

Others delegate some training objectives to local managers, each of whom is at liberty to develop the operation best suited to their particular context. Thus, at the European Travel Company, some work training courses are designed and rolled out locally.

Others again centralize training design but give each major institution or department the task of administering its deployment to a service provider of its choice.

Lastly, some corporations have drawn up precise rules to address these issues. In the case of L'Oréal, the training of the most senior middle managers is left to each country, while that of supervisory staff is handled by each of the major regions of the world and that of senior executives is managed at group level. As for training in the group's main policies that affect a lot of people, this is designed centrally and is usually run by local institutions according to methods of their choosing.

Naturally, in general, the more the training concerns "social skills," the more it has to adapt to local culture. The more it relates to senior management and to a corporation's key values and processes, the more it will be provided on a uniform basis.

All this clearly does not exhaust the list of preconditions for the success of a strategic training project.

As well as the need to communicate *meaning*, to ensure the *alignment* of different systems, and to involve key personnel (including *immediate line management* and *local managers*), there is a need to identify the other potential obstacles and sources of support. Among these, an often essential issue is the *work tools* placed at employees' disposal for the everyday application of their training.

Once these fundamental questions have been raised, you need to address another crucial and even more specific issue, that of *evaluation*. How can you lead a strategically important operation if you cannot measure its results?

The Evaluation of Strategic Training: A Path Strewn With Pitfalls

One of the main criticisms often made of training relates to the weakness of the economic results clearly accruing on completion of projects.

That is why the issue of evaluation is more of a burning issue than ever, particularly for programs where there is a lot at stake strategically.

Evaluation Is a Simple Matter … in Theory!

As long ago as the late 1950s, the American theorist Donald L. Kirkpatrick[2] claimed that there are four essential levels to the evaluation of training:

The *participants' perception* constitutes the first level of the evaluation.

Are they *satisfied* with their training? *In their view*, did it suit their needs? Do they *feel* that they have progressed? Do they *intend* to put at least some of the contents into practice?

Such perceptions can easily be measured by giving them a form to complete at the end of the session or a few days later.

The second level relates to the *benefits of the training*.

What have the employees really *learned* from it? What knowledge have they absorbed? Exactly what expertise and what new instincts have they acquired?

For knowledge, participants' claims are not enough: you need to use knowledge-based questionnaires or role play exercises to *test* what they have learned. For such tests to be beneficial, naturally you need to be able to compare their results with other, similar results obtained *prior to* training.

The third level of evaluation consists in observing *changes in working practices*.

Have employees actually *applied* what they learned during training? Do they take *initiatives* that they were not taking previously? Do they perform certain tasks *differently*? Have they changed their *behavior* in certain situations?

The fourth level concerns the *operational results achieved thanks to the training*.

Of course, the indicators to be examined depend on the subject of the training.

Has there been an increase in the *productivity* of the people trained? Has there been an improvement in *sales, profitability, or customer satisfaction*? Has there been a reduction in the number of *rejects, complaints, processing errors*, or *late deliveries*?

Another American, Dr Jack J. Phillips,[3] built on Kirkpatrick's research more recently by adding two further evaluation levels.

The fifth level consists in *isolating the specific impact of the training* on the operational outcomes achieved.

Where the pursuit of a strategic ambition is involved, training rarely exists in isolation. It is usually accompanied by other measures: raising middle management awareness, introducing new information systems, external advertising and internal promotional campaigns, competitions, changes in the way bonuses are calculated, etc.

It would therefore be absurd to credit training with all the results achieved.

Phillips therefore recommends that we identify each of the other elements that may have contributed to those results and then ask various stakeholders (e.g., middle managers and senior executives) to give a weighting to the role that they feel the different factors played in the progress identified.

Obviously, the resulting estimates are very approximate, but often less simplistic than drawing a direct connection between training and operational outcomes.

Lastly, the sixth and final level of evaluation involves *ROI*, which is calculated as a ratio of the economic results achieved compared to the overall cost of the training operation.

This means, firstly, attaching a financial value to the various operational outcomes attributed to the training and, secondly, evaluating the overall cost of that training, before comparing one figure to the other.

We can see that a program that cost $100,000 and that earned $130,000 has a ROI of 30%. You merely need to subtract the second figure from the first $(130 - 100 = 30)$ and then divide the result of that calculation by the second figure $(30 \div 100 = 0.3)$ before multiplying the result of that calculation by 100 $(0.3 \times 100 = 30)$ to obtain a ROI figure.

The logic of these different levels is overwhelming.

In practice, it is unrealistic to expect training to yield a ROI if it does not produce operational results and neither is it reasonable to expect it to produce results if people make no improvement in the way they work.

Likewise, improvements in the behavior of employees cannot be expected if those employees have learned nothing from their training, while people cannot be expected to acquire a solid grounding of skills if they are unhappy about the training contents, methods, or ambiance.

In addition, looking at things in reverse, these levels of evaluation offer an excellent approach when designing a strategy-oriented training project.

In the context of a strategic action plan, what results do we wish to achieve (in a specific field and within a given sphere of activity) and how are we to verify that we have actually achieved this?

To achieve those results, what changes must we see in our employees' working practices (priorities, methods, conduct) and how are we to verify that these are genuine changes?

Then, to achieve those changes, exactly what will those people have to learn and how will we ensure that they have actually learned it?

Lastly, to ensure that our employees do learn, what is required for them to "feel involved" during training, and what questions will we put to them after they have been trained to check that this objective has been achieved?

It is evident that the higher you go up these levels of evaluation, the closer you get to the true purposes of training from the perspective of the business and its strategy.

The problem is that, in practice, evaluating the contribution that training has made to strategy implementation is a real headache: apart from the standard questionnaire to assess satisfaction at the end of a session, the other levels of evaluation are often complex and costly to compile.

That is why both Kirkpatrick and Phillips consider that thought must be given as to how the resources allotted to training evaluation will be distributed.

Thus, in their view, *systematic use should be made of basic trainee satisfaction questionnaires but the evaluation of operational results must be reserved for those training sessions that have the most direct connection to strategy implementation.*

Put more simply, many corporations tend to neglect evaluation at level 3 (changes in conduct) and beyond, as it is deemed too difficult to handle.

Furthermore, level 1 evaluation (trainee satisfaction) is very often disparaged; it is seen as pretty meaningless and little use is made of it.

More and more frequently, the emphasis is therefore placed on level 2 evaluation (measurement of benefits), including the use of knowledge tests administered online, if possible with some measurement of the difference between knowledge prior to training and knowledge immediately after training.

Within certain organizations, level 6 evaluation (ROI) is also seen as an essential exercise: they feel the need to use it systematically to demonstrate that the *contribution training makes to the results achieved* greatly exceeds the *various resources (budgets, time)* invested in the latter.

This all seems to be plain common sense. However, the most effective businesses are developing an approach radically at odds with this. We shall now see why.

Trainee Satisfaction: A Greatly Underestimated Factor in Success

Everyone can think of examples of training courses that have aroused the enthusiasm of participants without ultimately yielding any significant progress.

For this reason, on-the-spot evaluation questionnaires have a poor reputation. Often disparagingly described as "smile tests," they are seen as easy for trainers to manipulate and poor at predicting the real use of training in promoting a strategy.

It is true that measurement instruments of this type are clearly inadequate.

It is also true that, for the trainer, the end-of-session questionnaire is of considerable importance, for reasons of self-esteem (of the trainer) and to garner hopefully favorable opinions (of the participants). It is therefore tempting for trainers to try to influence the participants' responses, maybe by exaggerating the value of the progress each person has supposedly made or by creating an emotional bond that would make trainees feel guilty about expressing any dissatisfaction.

However, contrary to general opinion, level 1 evaluation is absolutely crucial: participant satisfaction often plays a big part in determining the success of an operation.

First, this is because participant feedback is an absolutely indispensable source of continuous improvement for training designers and leaders.

Primarily, though, it is because enthusiastic participants clearly have a greater desire to put what they have learned during training into practice than skeptical or downright discontented employees.

Lastly, it is because word of mouth greatly influences the attitudes of other people who are likely to attend the program. In turn, their attitudes will play a decisive role in the atmosphere at future sessions, the support that people show for the corporation's messages, and the likelihood that they will apply the priorities, methods, and actions expected as part of the strategy.

It is therefore important to find reliable ways of gathering trainees' perceptions.

One advance that is now readily accessible is to collect evaluations *anonymously online the day after* the training, rather than by name on paper in the training room; the trainees are away from the physical proximity of the trainer and the group, and can add nuances and careful calibrations to their assessments.

Of course, the risk is that some of them will not take the time to respond to the questionnaire, once their time is again taken up by urgent everyday demands. That is why the solutions offered by the best training providers include an email and telephone reminder service, in practice allowing them to achieve response rates between 70% and 100%.

Another way of improving the relevance of on-the-spot evaluations is to ask employees questions about specific training objectives connected to the strategy.

For example: *"After completing this course, are you convinced of the need to promote comprehensive solutions to our partners?" "Are you even more determined to make a personal contribution to the success of the 'Customers First' project?" "Do you believe that collaborating with the other people involved in this project will be easier from now on?" "Do you feel capable of using the new software straightaway in order to process your casework?"* etc.

Questions that focus on the training itself (quality of group leadership, appropriateness of methods, etc.) are beneficial, but those concerning the individual trainee, their comprehension of what is at stake, their trust in their own ability to act, and their intentions to put learning into practice are even more useful.

Evaluating the Benefits of Training: Occasionally Essential, Often Counterproductive

As we have stated, there is currently a trend for the evaluation of the benefits of training to become systematic.

The lessons learned can take various forms: knowledge retention, mastery of expertise, acceptance of attitudes. In the case of a training course for bank counter staff, *knowledge* may include those customer requests that must be referred for management approval. *Expertise* may concern how to get a customer interested in a simple, special-offer deal and how to clinch a sale. An example of *attitude* is seeing every customer as important and any expression of discontent as justified, in principle.

Nobody would complain if you were to check that a medical rep had properly learned the correct doses and list of contraindications attached to a new product for infants, or that an airline pilot was fully *au fait* with the various stages in the emergency landing procedure.

It is obvious that, in such cases, the fact that trainees might say they are satisfied at the end of the course cannot be sufficient for the training to be declared a success: level 2 evaluation (training benefits) is essential in this case.

Unfortunately, however, such evaluation often proves not only pointless but even counterproductive.

We should start by saying that the practical impossibility of measuring *attitudes* and difficulty of accurately evaluating *expertise* in work situations naturally leads us to prioritize either training room simulations or the evaluation of *knowledge* alone.

Yet such an approach suffers from three flaws.

First, in medicine, for example, grades achieved in finals exams are not a reliable guide to the effectiveness of the treatments that doctors subsequently prescribe. A better indication is the patient's recovery from illness which testifies to the doctor's diagnostic ability.

In most professions there is no positive correlation between extra *knowledge* and the extent to which a strategy is implemented or even the extent to which performance improves. In rare cases (e.g., certain sales forces), a *negative correlation* has even been found: the greater the product knowledge, the lower the sales, because the sales reps take refuge in technical jargon instead of focusing on the customer's expectations and motivations.

In contrast, there are training courses where participants *learn* little but where a significant improvement in working practices is generated, maybe thanks to greater staff awareness or motivation.

Second, using tests to evaluate training (and therefore, indirectly, the trainer) leads, paradoxically but inevitably, to a *deterioration in the operational effectiveness of the training*.

In practice, as demonstrated by Robert Bjork, Professor of Psychology at UCLA and a specialist in memory and learning, the teaching methods that allow for the optimum success rate in tests are very different from those that facilitate successful implementation in a work context.

To increase test success rate, a trainer has to *repeat* the *same information* in the *same way* many times, to ask trainees to complete *simple* exercises in a *stable* environment and to provide *instant* feedback, all within the *shortest possible* timescale.

In contrast, the ability to put things into practice on the ground requires the trainer to address the subject from *different* angles, to get trainees to complete *increasingly complex* exercises in *a variety* of contexts, to provide regular but *not instant* feedback (allowing the trainee time to assess their own performance) and, crucially, to *space* training sessions out to provide opportunities for experimentation. In short, these are precisely the things that the trainer should avoid if tests are used to evaluate training.

Lastly, the *time needed* to complete knowledge tests at the beginning and end of training courses is generally taken at the expense of practical coaching, despite this being much more useful from the perspective of implementation.

Clearly, all this should not lead us to exclude level 2 evaluation.

It is just that such evaluation must not *assume excessive importance* in the management of strategic training projects or in the time that people devote to their skills development programs.

Where it is important to measure *knowledge* is when *knowledge* acquisition really is crucial to the implementation of new working practices.

There is only really any justification for evaluating the *expertise* acquired during training, a difficult and time-consuming task, if provision is made for corrective measures: for example, if extra sessions are laid on for people who have not yet mastered the skills required.

Otherwise, it is more worthwhile to concentrate on evaluating the changes made in the workplace.

The Central Issue Is the Evaluation of Change

Ultimately, this is the precise level where training plays its role in the implementation of a strategy.

Beforehand, the positive perceptions of trainees and even the acquisition of new skills are merely means to an end. They are of little benefit if they do not produce any identifiable change in the way in which employees do their work.

Afterward, achieving operational results and measuring a positive ROI are highly desirable outcomes, of course. Yet they are generally only partly dependent on training, so they are difficult to identify with precision.

There are certainly a limited number of circumstances in which it is possible to measure the economic impact of a training program perfectly.

For example, a major banking chain wanted to boost the profitability of its property loans. In particular, it needed to help its sales people to negotiate better with each customer on issues such as offering a more favorable lending rate in exchange for reducing administration fees, or abolishing penalties for early repayment, etc.

Having been seduced "on paper" by a particular sales method, the bank opted to train a fifth of its branches, at random, right across the country.

There were other ongoing initiatives to boost the profitability of property loans: PR campaigns, new sales support, improved segmentation of customer portfolios, etc. But these initiatives were identical at every branch.

Over a 6-month period, the banking chain as a whole posted a rise of 0.15 points in the profitability of its property loans. Those branches where training had been provided made significantly more progress, up 0.65 points on average.

Without question, the disparity in performance was due to the training alone. It was therefore possible to measure the (clearly very high) ROI from that training, before deciding to introduce the operation generally across the nation as a whole.

In other circumstances, corporations have been able to accurately measure the impact of training on nonfinancial performance indicators: error rates, customer satisfaction, staff commitment, etc.

Astonishingly, however, of all the multitude of training projects introduced within corporations, such examples remain the exception. Many firms hesitate to specifically test their training on a sample of their target group before introducing it on a universal basis. Why?

Maybe they question the impact of the initiative and are put off by the fixed costs of developing and updating the program, which are difficult to offset against a test group.

Alternatively, maybe they are convinced that the operation will be a success and want to move forward as quickly as possible. It is true that the bank described above incurred an opportunity cost of 0.5% on its property loans at 80% of its branches for a grand period of 6 months!

Thus, the results posted on completion of "strategic" training operations are generally to be taken with a pinch of salt, as official PR credits them with successes that are really only partially attributable to them.

Another essential reservation regarding the measurement of ROI concerns the risk of slippage in the general management of training operations.

Some operations do generate more direct and immediate economic benefits than others. This is the case, notably, for training courses that focus on the negotiation of commercial margins (sales or purchases) and on action to identify savings.

This does not mean that such initiatives are always the most appropriate. When Southwest Airlines trains its personnel in company values and in interdepartmental cooperation to promote customer service, ROI is impossible to calculate and doubtless sometimes nonexistent. Yet, for almost 40 years, training of this type has allowed that corporation to pursue a strategy that has brought it unparalleled success in the aviation sector.

That is why, despite the obvious benefits of measuring the economic results of strategic training, *evaluating changes in working practices* is generally a more relevant indicator of the impact of an initiative.

Evaluation of this type is especially important when the training is directly connected to strategic ambitions, when it concerns large groups and particularly people in direct customer contact and when it involves issues of *compliance*.

Training alone certainly does not determine how people act in their working environments either.

Other important elements play a part: the instructions, but above all the example set by their line manager, the pressure to conform created by the attitudes of colleagues, the consistency of evaluation criteria and, where applicable, performance-related pay, help or hindrance from work tools, other competing priorities, etc.

Yet these elements do have to be *anticipated*, taken into account and addressed when preparing and introducing a training project.

Exactly how should the changes generated by training be evaluated?

Schematically, there are three potential approaches.

The most basic approach is to ask the employees themselves and their immediate line manager about it sometime after the training.

Certain online evaluation systems automate that procedure. Immediately after being trained, employees record their own assessments, but above all they also record three or four key points of their action plan. A few months later, they are asked (again online and anonymously) to indicate to what extent they have or have not carried out the decisions that they themselves recorded. The line manager is also asked about the nature and scale of the changes observed in their staff members after training. For major projects, the corporation therefore has access to a fairly accurate image of the impact of training on behavior at work.

A more sophisticated evaluation method is to put questions to people whose work brings them into contact with each trainee: line manager, peers, subordinates, internal or external partners, and customers.

When conducted before and after training, 360-degree assessments offers a more objective view of the progress achieved, especially with regard to factors involving personal conduct and interpersonal relations.

Lastly, certain subjects of strategic importance justify the completion of thorough-going audits by third parties.

For example, in the context of a major training project designed to improve service quality on each of its sites, a large service company recently launched an initiative that involves awarding *accreditations* on the company's top performers. Each site manager who has been trained gets ready for a rigorous audit carried out by a qualified third party. The audit allows them to measure precise progress based on criteria for the application of service and management standards compared to the comprehensive diagnostics completed a few months earlier.

In the case of points of sale, visits from "mystery customers" also allow for monitoring of changes in working practices and on-the-job behaviour.

To conclude this subsection devoted to evaluation, we must stress how much is at stake and the need to be cautious of spurious miracle solutions: knowledge evaluation, measurement of ROI, etc.

Corporations can make enormous improvements in their collection and use of participants' *perceptions*, including through the use of the latest online systems.

In certain cases, they can also measure progress in *knowledge* and in certain types of *expertise*, provided that this does not curtail productive training time. It is also subject to the proviso that it must not lead trainers to focus on "passing the test" rather than achieving real-life success.

They must certainly try to do better at monitoring the *changes* that people make in their working practices. Here again, modern online systems allow them to collect reliable data. For crucial issues, 360-degree assessments and audits can contribute to more sophisticated measures that are simultaneously more stimulating and more accurate.

Lastly, in certain rarer cases, they can measure *operational or even financial results directly and unequivocally connected to training* or can even use them to calculate *ROI*.

For example, in the case of the global electrical engineering company, all the "learning and development solutions" teams worldwide were trained in Jack Phillips' approach to evaluation, as described earlier. The ultimate aim is to see satisfaction surveys conducted among the customers of in-house training services being perceived as a strategic investment and not as a cost.

The Emergence of "Cost-Effective Training"

As we have seen, the measurement of ROI in training is—and will largely remain—an old chestnut.

On the other hand, the need to *train more people more effectively and more cheaply* is set to become even more pressing: even though it is a tool for the implementation of a strategy, training does not have an unlimited call on corporate budgets.

In this area, the progress that can be made is spectacular.

It is important to fully understand the mechanics of training costs, in order to identify the levers that will allow you to drastically improve your cost effectiveness.

Training Costs Are Not Necessarily What You Think They Are

In general, training costs have a bad reputation: deemed to be unnecessarily high, they are assumed to be incurred without proper control and to usually yield no measurable ROI.

Strategic training projects have the disadvantage of a high profile, given the high stakes involved and also the large numbers of people affected. This means that they attract, if not criticism then at least doubt, as to whether they are worth what they cost.

Training is expensive, both directly and indirectly.

We shall not address in detail the issue of *indirect costs*, which can be high given the extent of government red tape surrounding training.

Nevertheless, we need to remember that, as well as the costs of training departments, they include the working time of all those people involved in the management of such projects: purchasing, accounts, operations, and staff managers brought onboard by steering committees, etc.

Taking the hypothesis of a "standard" project, we shall see that, schematically, there are *three major types of direct costs* associated with training.

Of course, it is the *teaching costs* that occur to us first, costs that are partly fixed but mainly variable.

Fixed teaching costs accrue from the development of training products and systems: initial research, the design of case studies and teaching aids, the production of e-learning modules, etc. These costs are set against the project as a whole.

Variable teaching costs are principally connected to trainers and to teaching documents.

External organizers and consultants invoice their fees, which can be expensive, while in-house trainers generally involve a lower theoretical daily cost but generate indirect costs (management, premises, equipment, social benefits, etc.) and risks of internal disputes.

The costs of teaching documents are proportional to the number of participants, whereas those of trainers depend primarily on the number of groups to be trained.

Lastly, account needs to be taken of the fees invoiced by external service providers for project management and for passing their expertise on to the various trainers responsible for the work, potentially in many different countries and in many different languages. Those costs are broadly, if not exactly, proportional to the scale of the operation.

Logistical costs include rooms and their audiovisual equipment as well as participants' travel, subsistence, and accommodation costs. Of course, the scale of these costs will largely depend on the geographical dispersal of the trainees.

Lastly, *opportunity costs* correspond to work that is not done while the employees are being trained: customers not visited by reps, breakdowns not repaired by technicians, etc. Conventionally, account is also taken of the payroll costs of employees while they are undergoing training.

Let us take the example of a corporation operating through a large business unit whose strategy requires it to rapidly redirect the work of 3,000 people, scattered across 10 countries, from selling products to selling solutions.

Let us assume that a training project is prepared based on an absolutely standard model: the sales person and their line managers will receive 3 days of training in groups of 12 on courses developed and led by an external service provider.

Let us also assume that designing the training courses requires a budget of $90,000, given the customized nature of the training, and the number and quality of resources expected for such a major project, as well as the many different versions to be prepared for the various categories of sales person and managers affected by the project.

Furthermore, 25 trainers are to be seconded to run 750 training days. Each of them has to devote 3 days to preparing their own teaching aids for this training, which represents a specific budget of $112,500.

The costs of adapting all this for international use amount to $10,000 per country: document translation, dubbing of audiovisual media, modification of case studies, etc.

Running the courses accounts for 750 days, while project management accounts for a fixed percentage of 10% of those man-days.

Based on the daily price of $1,500 and a cost of $25 per teaching aid, total *teaching costs* amount to $1,645,000.

If we assume that expenditure on room hire and lunch totals $100 per participant per day, as do the cumulative costs of travel and accommodation, the *logistical costs* amount to $1,500,000.

Lastly, based on the average payroll costs of $300 per working day, corresponding to an average gross salary of about $43,000 per annum, the *opportunity costs* come to $2,700,000.

In total, the direct costs are $5,845,000, equivalent to just under $2,000 per participant.

Proportionally, *teaching costs per se* account for 28.1% of this sum and *logistical costs* account for 25.7%. *Opportunity costs*, namely the payroll costs of the people trained, represent about 46.2% of the burden, or almost half of the total.

Naturally, these proportions may vary depending on the characteristics of the projects and the nature of the groups concerned: for middle managers and executives, opportunity costs often account for well over half of all direct costs.

In general, it is still true that for a major training operation, the costs connected to the trainees' pay amount to at least 40% of the direct cost, with the logistical burden and expenditure on external trainers and consultants each often representing just over a quarter of the net total.

A drastic reduction in training costs requires action on these three items. The issue is discovering how to do this.

Bright Ideas That Aren't

This concern to reduce training costs is nothing new.

Unfortunately, until recently, the methods used by the training "cost killers" (training institutions and businesses) would lead to a decline in training quality even greater than that in training costs.

The methods that seem the most obvious at first sight often create havoc in practice.

The first consists in reducing the number of people eligible for training. After all, why train 3,000 people when training 300 line managers might suffice? That way, they can explain to their staff the changes that are to be made to their habits and how to achieve the results expected.

A variant on this method is to extend the deployment of the training across several budget years. In the previous chapter, we saw that this was the best and surest means of discouraging people from putting the desired behavior into practice.

Another poor option is to reduce the duration of the training without changing its objectives or adapting its teaching methods. This almost always leads to a reduction in the time devoted to practical coaching, but we have seen that practical coaching is the most crucial element in effective training.

In other circumstances, to limit travel costs, firms may cram work due to occupy several session into a single long session, thereby eliminating the potential for gradual implementation and short bursts of "over-learning."

Alternatively, to reduce the number of sessions, we might add a few extra course members to each group. If no change is made in teaching methods, this generates a more than proportional reduction in training effectiveness for each course member.

Other, equally counterproductive methods involve teaching costs more directly.

Saving time on program design and development inevitably leads to a decline in the quality and relevance of the service provided to employees.

Reducing the time that the various trainers spend learning about the specific context that they are working in is bound to mean sacrificing some of the accuracy of their responses to participants.

Negotiating a reduction in trainers' rates will lead, by necessity and over time, to your courses being allocated to people who are less qualified or less highly motivated.

We could continue to cite further examples of cost-cutting methods that lead, in reality, to a further decline in the training cost-effectiveness ratio.

The question is whether there are any means of *drastically cutting the costs* of a strategic training project, while achieving *even greater effectiveness* than that obtained from standard programs?

The answer is: yes, there certainly is, provided that you remove certain taboos and challenge various training paradigms.

Several leading corporations are showing us the way forward.

The Efficient Reduction of Training Time

Naturally, the number of hours and days that each employee spends on training largely determines total project cost; it impacts directly and proportionally on opportunity costs, on design, management and teaching costs, as well as on most logistical costs (rooms, subsistence, and accommodation).

Yet if we analyze the value of the time spent on training, we discover that a lot of this is wasted.

Firstly, during a traditional training session, *productive time* represents just a fraction of the total time that each participant spends on the training.

Round-table exercises are generally pretty unproductive: each individual waits for their turn without really learning from their peers.

The trainer's *talks* partly cover subjects that some course members are already familiar with and partly cover issues that only concern a few of them directly. These talks are often *slowed down* by discussions with the group, during which one or two participants hog the floor and repeatedly intervene without saying anything of interest to the rest.

The people we are describing as *participants* are, in truth, *spectators* during many phases of training: observing exercises carried out by others, the pitiful returns on small group work, during which various spokespeople present more or less identical and obvious findings.

Secondly, this regrettably limited *productive time* does not always offer a *high yield* when it comes to learning skills.

In particular, the exercises are generally complex. They take a long time to prepare for and are partly devoted to remembering particular details that serve no purpose outside the context of the training course. Completing the exercise brings so many parameters into play that it complicates subsequent analysis of the lessons to be drawn. In addition, the practical impossibility of completing the same exercise several times has a considerable impact on the ability of individuals to make practical use of what have they have learned in the workplace.

It is possible to greatly reduce the duration of training courses, while increasing their effectiveness, if you change your teaching methods.

In 2008, for the worldwide launch of its first loyalty card, a leading hotel chain needed to train 15,000 managers and receptionists. These employees had to learn to understand how the card worked, how loyalty points were calculated, and what computer procedures were required to register subscribers. This was achieved successfully within half a day.

When L'Oréal trained its recruitment managers in 2009, the duration of the training was reduced to 1 day and proved highly effective.

There are three preconditions for the efficient reduction of training time.

The first involves ensuring that the participants are better *prepared*.

By giving participants easy access to the basic content required, perhaps through e-learning modules, a business allows each individual to prepare at their own pace, according to their own needs, and often via mobile terminals while otherwise occupied: during a train journey, while waiting for an appointment, etc.

Most of the trainer's talks and the frequently time-wasting interruptions by participants can be entirely dispensed within the classroom sessions.

In L'Oréal's case, thanks to some brief and stimulating preparatory work, the participants arrived at the course with an awareness of the corporation's policy on talent, the key points of the process, and the division of recruitment roles between line managers and HR as well as the key values to be promoted.

The second precondition relates to the *way in which group sessions are run*.

By eliminating round-table exercises, drastically reducing the number of group discussions in favor of very short and increasingly difficult exercises and focusing content on the essential objectives that are to be achieved (what Americans call "low-fat training"!), training productivity can be greatly increased, when it comes to practical application in the workplace.

Lastly, the third precondition concerns the *cascading* of the training.

A short training course leading to information being actively passed on by line management is often more worthwhile than a long course with no follow-up. "Kits" that allow pretrained line managers to lead short sequences of "refresher sessions" at weekly or monthly meetings have a considerable impact on effectiveness.

Likewise, practical tools that allow you to either revisit key points of the training through e-learning or to directly apply the content of the training in a work situation are often at least as useful as an extra day's training.

It *is* possible to reduce training time.

Changing Group Size

Some teaching costs are proportional to the number of groups and not the number of participants. This mainly applies to group leadership costs.

As we have already seen in detail, it is possible (and often even desirable) to greatly increase group size in certain training situations, provided of course that you adopt teaching methods especially designed for large numbers.

For example, with the help of our London team, Tesco employed exceptionally dynamic methods to train hundreds of tech support advisors (a new position) for its British supermarkets, in groups of 50. Tesco Tech Support Managing Director Rod Brown believes that "this approach allowed us not only to build a very high level of skills and commitment among our technicians, … but also to save on the cost of a traditional training programme by 30%."

Paradoxically, such groups also allow you to largely offset the extra cost connected to running practice sessions in very small groups, as we saw in the case of Onet.

Cutting the Costs of International Deployment

For many projects, it is possible to cut deployment costs by investing a little more—and a little more wisely—in initial design work. This requires the development of tools and resources that are easily transferable and adaptable to trainers and trainees from different countries or institutions.

The Leadership Academy of the above-mentioned electrical engineering company offers high-quality curricula blending e-learning, *web seminars*, classroom training, coaching by line management, etc., while significantly optimizing costs. Prior to the creation of this academy, each country was obliged to invest in the preparation of content and in educational engineering, in order to develop services whose objectives were very similar, but whose effectiveness was less consistent.

Sometimes, it is the use of a particular technology that generates savings on deployment.

For example, the Training Academy of a global leader in the automobile industry, responsible for the training of the group's networks worldwide, was able to make considerable savings thanks to 3D.

For training in new vehicle maintenance, the time taken for local trainers to grasp content represents a major cost. In addition, the technical training manuals have to be translated into dozens of languages: translation costs alone account for up to 30% of the network's total training budgets.

By producing 3D video animations, the Training Academy was able to drastically reduce this translation budget and the time taken to prepare local trainers.

Eliminating the Cost of Pointless Special Developments

Customization is generally a precondition for training to be effective, as individuals struggle to transpose learning from one context to another.

"Off-the-shelf" training products are well suited to very general training, such as courses giving access to a job or leading to career qualifications. They can also suit highly qualified people who are used to juggling abstract concepts or capable of quickly transposing examples from one context to another.

For other kinds of training, the vocabulary and examples used, the exercises and even the images must be adapted to the world in which the trainee works. There is nothing more ridiculous, for example, than a foreign teaching video dubbed in broken English, depicting people in outdated clothing, especially if the action takes place in settings quite different from the workplace of the prospective trainees.

That is why those 35,000 employees invited to find out about the green economy through the serious game "The expert within" enjoyed the benefits of a high-quality product whose content was specifically adapted to their employer's needs.

Schematically, there are two ways of obtaining a teaching solution of this sort.

The first is to develop a fully customized product.

In that case, the scenario, graphics, sequencing and image production, special effects, musical soundtrack, and voice recordings are produced especially for that particular business. Likewise, documentary editing is done specially by a team of experts.

Inevitably, these multiple operations, which are already inherently costly and time consuming, give rise to debate, alterations, and additions prior to final approval. All this generates massive investment.

Yet this solution is often the universal option of choice.

The project manager sees it as a means of benefiting from a unique "tailor-made" product perfectly adapted to the specific needs of their business, its objectives and its prospective trainees.

Similarly, the service provider has a clear economic interest in selling a sophisticated solution rather than a simple, off-the-shelf product.

In some cases, a fully customized product is indeed the only possible response to a particular need.

However, the second option is becoming more accessible. This consists in *taking maximum advantage of existing tools, developments, and content* by specially designing only those extra elements that are really needed.

In the case of the corporation that wanted to train 35,000 people in the green economy, *L'expertise dans la peau* ("The Expert Within")[2] was a "template" designed to work with any kind of customized teaching content. The imagery and music, most of the voices off, the sequencing and the array of educational exercises had *already* been developed, tested, and perfected. All that remained was to insert those elements referring to the specific content of that project.

Unlike standard serious games that oblige the corporation alone to bear the heavy development costs, solutions of this type are clearly much more economical, but they come with at least the same quality of outcome and an educational content that is customized to the same extent. They can cost up to five times less.

More generally, the cost of many projects escalates unnecessarily through pointless development work. *Customized content* need not mean *fully customized development*. The best solutions combine existing resources and special adaptations.

Making Some of the Training Time Directly Productive

As we have seen, *opportunity costs* represent by far the greatest individual cost of any strategic training project.

It is assumed that while employees are in training, they are not doing their work.

Does that always need to be true?

When Sodexo polishes up its managers' excellence in winning customer loyalty, the sessions are partly devoted to preparatory work and even rehearsals for scheduled meetings with the trainees' main customers.

The best way of learning is often to practice. Thus, in many cases, some of the training time can be transformed into directly productive time: people *do some of their work during their training*.

That time should then be deducted from calculations analyzing specific project costs.

Increasing the Number of Zero-Cost Educational Initiatives

Another way of boosting the training cost-effectiveness ratio is to add educational value to everyday work situations outside the administrative scope of training.

This can be when middle managers use some of their time at *regular meetings* to run short "refresher sessions" or use some of the time spent one-to-one with each staff member to do some operational coaching.

It can also involve the use of *major prescheduled corporate events* (annual executive convention, seasonal launch meetings, sales conferences, head office road shows, etc.) to "host" short training sequences.

Practical Application

In the case cited in Section 3.1, the training project represents a direct cost of $5.8m when it is run according to a traditional format.

Let us now imagine that we had applied the principles described earlier.

Before taking part in group training, each participant uses cutting-edge self-tuition tools to get up to speed. A budget of $50,000 is devoted to their development.

Classroom training is reduced to 2 days, instead of 3. One day is run in groups of sixty trainees by two trainers, one of whom is an internationally recognized expert, whose daily fees are three times higher than those of other training leaders, and this session is attended by senior company managers. The second day is mainly run in small groups of six, with one trainer per group at a daily rate of $1,500. An exceptionally charismatic leader, costing $2,000 per day, presides over all the sessions.

Through the intelligent use of existing resources, design costs are limited to $75,000, including the production of resources easily adaptable to different countries and institutions.

Another budget of $20,000 allows supervisors to be provided with a set of multimedia resources, so that they can run refresher sessions during meetings.

This is certainly a much higher quality solution than the traditional model, and most importantly it is more productive. Advance self-tuition, high-quality aids, expert trainers, highly motivating sessions, personalized guidance for all, and the involvement of line management: everything about it is better.

Yet its overall cost is just $4,282,000 or *26.7% less than* the first option!

Despite improved effectiveness, teaching costs have been cut by 4%. Most importantly, though, the *opportunity costs* have been reduced by *a third* and *logistical costs*, which offer little added value, are down by *40%*.

	Traditional model	"Cost-effective" model	Difference in $	Difference as %
Number of people to be trained	3,000	3,000		
Duration of sessions	3	2		
Number of people per group	12	60		
Number of groups	250	50		
Leaders	–	–		
Number of trainers per session	1	10		
Number of days trainers in attendance	3	1		
(Assumed) total number of trainers	25	20		

(Continued)

(*Continued*)

	Traditional model	"Cost-effective" model	Difference in $	Difference as %
Daily cost per trainer	1,500	1,500		
Number of international experts per session	–	1		
Number of days expert in attendance	–	1		
Daily cost per international expert	4,500	4,500		
Number of large group leaders	–	1		
Number of days large group leader present	–	2		
Daily cost of large group leader	–	2,000		
Direct staffing cost per session	4,500	23,500		
Subtotal: Direct cost of staffing sessions	1,125,000	1,175,000	50,000	4
Number of days for training design	60	40		
Daily cost of design	1,500	1,500		
Training design cost	90,000	60,000		
Development of tools for multiplier effect	–	15,000		
Management tool kit	–	20,000		

	Traditional model	"Cost-effective" model	Difference in $	Difference as %
E-learning self-tuition	–	50,000		
Subtotal: Design costs	90,000	145,000	55,000	61
Trainer preparation time	3	1		
Trainer preparation cost	112,500	30,000		
(Estimated) costs of international adaptation	100,000	20,000		
Subtotal: Transfer costs	212,500	50,000	–162,500	–76
Project management	142,750	137,000		
Teaching documentation ($25 per person)	75,000	75,000		
Subtotal: Other teaching costs	217,750	212,000	–5,750	–3
TOTAL TEACHING COSTS	**1,645,250**	**1,582,000**	**–63,250**	**–4**
Average daily pay cost	300	300		
Pay costs	2,700,000	1,800,000		
TOTAL OPPORTU-NITY COSTS	**2,700,000**	**1,800,000**	**–900,000**	**–33**
Daily cost of room and lunch per person	100	100		
Subtotal: Room and lunch costs	900,000	600,000		

(Continued)

(*Continued*)

	Traditional model	"Cost-effective" model	Difference in $	Difference as %
Nightly subsistence/accommodation costs per person	100	100		
Subtotal: Subsistence/accommodation cost	600,000	300,000		
TOTAL LOGISTICAL COSTS	1,500,000	900,000	–600,000	–40
OVERALL TOTAL	5,845,250	4,282,000	–1,563,250	–26.7
Total cost per person	1,948	1,427	–521	–26.7
Teaching costs as a proportion of total	28.1%	36.9%		
Opportunity costs as a proportion of total	46.2%	42.0%		
Logistical costs as a proportion of total	25.7%	21.0%		

For other projects, the differences may be even greater.

It can be seen that we are talking not about "low-cost training" but about *cost-effective training*: it is a case of fully meeting the strategic objectives laid down on the best possible economic terms.

To conclude this chapter, training is a profession for grocers as well as strategists, ... but there's a bit more to it than that.

It is a profession for strategists as it requires a fully comprehensive awareness of the implications and an in-depth analysis of the objectives and preconditions for the success of training operations that are essential to the success of the business.

It is a profession for grocers as each pound invested in training must be shown to serve a purpose.

There's a bit more to it than that because it is now possible to achieve breakthroughs in your cost-effectiveness ratio, even for, and especially including, large-scale operations.

Key Points to Remember

- At company level, three fundamental questions arise: To what extent is each strategic priority effectively supported by training? What proportion of your financial resources for training is actually allocated to the deployment of the strategy? What proportion of your training personnel devote their time to tasks meeting the needs of that strategy?
- At project level, you need to do in-depth work on the objectives of the training project: connection with strategy, groups concerned, behavior expected, measurable results anticipated, economic implications, indicators of success. Then there are the preconditions for success, which specifically involve the meaning given to the project, the alignment of the corporation's priorities and systems with its strategy, the involvement of key people (top management, immediate line management and local managers), and the work tools.
- Any strategic training project must give rise to in-depth evaluation.
  - It is desirable to gather participants' perceptions anonymously, online and away from the training room.
  - Measuring progress in knowledge and some expertise is useful, but must not divert the training from its real goal, namely application of learning in a real-work situation.
  - It is crucial to monitor the changes that people make in their working practices: through online questionnaires directed at trainees and their line managers, and through 360-degree assessments or audits.
  - In certain circumstances, it is possible to measure operational results directly connected to training, or even to calculate ROI.

- It is possible to pursue major training projects in a "cost-effective" manner by using various levers.
  - Using innovative teaching methods to reduce training time and increase average group size.
  - Designing training in such a way as to reduce the cost of adapting it and of rolling it out internationally.
  - Eliminating irrelevant special development costs.
  - Making some of the training time directly productive.
  - Shifting some of the teaching work to the operational field.

Recommendations

The training connected to the implementation of our strategy ...	Yes!	More or less ...	Not yet
Does it accurately cover *each strategic priority*, both centrally and at the level of the various business units?			
Does it represent a *significant and growing proportion* of our total training expenditure?			
Does it mainly involve our training teams in high value-added tasks: listening to needs, leading, evaluating impact, etc.			
Is it systematically the subject of in-depth consideration of the groups concerned, the behavior expected, the measurable outcomes anticipated, and the indicators of success?			
Does it always give rise to exhaustive analysis of the *preconditions for success*: meaning given to project, alignment of priorities and systems, involvement of top management, line management, and local managers, work tools, etc.?			
Do employees evaluate it anonymously, online, and away from the training room?			
Do employees evaluate it based on questions relating to the *specific objectives* of the project in connection with the strategy?			
... and on questions about commitment to the strategy?			

… and on their intentions to put it into practice?			
Does it give rise to the measurement of progress in *knowledge* and in certain types of *expertise*, without thereby sacrificing productive training time?			
Does it use an online system to coolly evaluate the nature and scale of the changes that trainees have made in their working practices?			
For the most crucial subjects, does it give rise to 360-degree assessments or audits entrusted to third parties, in order to evaluate the improvements achieved through training?			
Where possible, do we measure the operational or even financial results that the training generates directly?			
… or do we even calculate a precise return on investment?			
Is it designed to reduce the duration of sessions through "real" solutions: advance self-tuition, focus on limited objectives, suitable teaching methods, cascading, and subsequent refresher sessions?			
Does it optimize group size (large group sessions and coaching in very small groups)?			
Is it arranged so as to keep trainer preparation and international adaptation costs to a minimum?			
Does it incorporate directly productive training time, during which the trainees do some of their work?			
Does it allow an educational value to be given to "nontraining" work situations (monthly meetings, line manager support, etc.)?			
Does it use major prescheduled company events?			
Does it use innovative teaching methods facilitating a reduction in the duration of sessions and an increase in group size?			
Is it designed to *keep international deployment and adaptation costs* to a minimum?			

(Continued)

(*Continued*)

Does it make maximum use of existing resources in order to *avoid unnecessary development costs*?			
Does it include *directly productive working time*, during which trainees do their "real" work?			
Does it include certain educational work completed during operational work in "*nontraining time*"?			

CHAPTER 8

Conclusion: Gazing into Our Crystal Ball

What Does the Future Hold for Strategic Training?

The decade from 2002 to 2012 witnessed some spectacular changes that few people could have predicted. The BRICs (Brazil, Russia, India, and China) racked up 67 businesses in the 2010 classification of the world's top corporations, compared to just four decade earlier. The iPod, iTunes, and the iPhone created enormous new markets, promoting Apple to the world's most admired company. And Web 2.0, a completely unknown concept 10 years before, won over *billions* of users. Facebook, Twitter, and other social-networking sites became household names, seemingly overnight.

Lacking a crystal ball and supernatural powers, we would do well to exercise caution when it comes to economic forecasting. Nevertheless, alive to emerging trends, we can try to formulate a few hypotheses about the way in which businesses will use training to support their strategies over the coming years.

The amazing development of the market in intelligent mobile terminals, such as smartphones, electronic tablets, and netbooks, will doubtless have a great impact in the business world. We can imagine that, one day, strategy will partly be rolled out through tiny doses of training lasting fewer than 3 minutes. "Just-in-time" content will be readily available, the number of networked serious games will multiply, and special apps, with names such as "expert locator" or "virtual manager" proliferating.

Time spent commuting or waiting in a customer's reception therefore represents a niche training market that mobile technology is bringing within reach but which awaits exploitation. However, training will find itself in competition with other program providers seeking to capture the "free brain time" of employees. These include news media, producers of video games, and distributors of digital films, not to mention other business services or even organizations representing employees. Training will therefore need to radically boost its attractiveness. The marketing of training remains a skill yet to be explored.

Platforms allowing people to develop DIY training software will continue to increase rapidly and to become simpler and more accessible. Today it is already possible to design your own e-learning module, whereas just 5 years ago this would have required a team of graphic designers and software developers. Teachers will construct e-learning tools for their pupils, likewise, parents will do so for their children, and business experts will do the same for new recruits. Those with a passion for any subject will take similar action in their own interest and the interest of others.

Almost all these tools will be available on the Web, just as videos are available on YouTube. This means that numerous, generally free or low-cost teaching aids will soon be accessible online. Within large corporations, a similar phenomenon should materialize, with a whole range of freely accessible in-house content in various educational formats. This will offer all employees the opportunity to train at their own pace, using the methods that suit them best.

As a result of all this, traditional training packages might logically fall into decline, although this is far from certain given the rapid growth in needs. If that is the case, physical gatherings will be all the more important due to their rarity. The boundaries between training and events, teaching and communications, and coaching and mobilization could become blurred.

Ultimately, though, training methods count for little. It is underlying trends that really matter. The best corporations will understand more clearly than ever that the success of their strategies relies on people. They will invest with greater determination and efficiency in skills development, commitment, and a common culture. Gradually they will gauge their employees' potential, at present greatly underexploited. Let there be no doubt, training is a profession of the future. Companies will begin to grasp the importance of training and to embrace the modern methods and approaches to it.

Notes

Chapter 1

1. Lyall (2009, July 31).
2. Magretta (2011).
3. Cable (2007).

Chapter 2

1. Ericsson (2009).
2. Ericsson (1996).
3. Letter to the author.

Chapter 3

1. Wagner (2006).
2. Buckingham (2005).

Chapter 4

1. The Future of Management, Harvard Business School Press (2007).
2. de Bono (2010).
3. Pink (2008).
4. Bandura (1997).
5. Seligman (2006).
6. Raynor, Ahmed, and Henderson (2009).
7. Gardner (2011).
8. Campbell (2003).
9. Trompenaars, Hampden-Turner, and Brealey (2012).

Chapter 5

1. Granovetter (1973).
2. Dunbar (1998).
3. Mintzberg, Ahlstrand, and Lampel (2010).
4. Gourville (2006).

Chapter 6

1. Alfred (1969).
2. *Evaluation of Evidence-Based Practices in Online Learning, A Meta-Analysis and Review of Online Learning Studies*, US Department of Education, 2009, étude disponible en ligne.

Chapter 7

1. Drucker (2008).
2. Kirkpatrick and Kirkpatrick (2006).
3. Phillips (2003).

References

Bandura, A. (1997). *Self efficacy in changing societies*. New York: Cambridge University Press.

Buckingham, M. (2005). *First, break all the rules*. New York: Simon & Schuster.

Cable, D. (2007). *Change to strange*. Upper Saddle River, NJ: Prentice Hall.

Campbell, L., Campbell, B., & Dickinson, D. (2003). *Teaching and learning through multiple intelligences*. Upper Saddle River, NJ: Pearson.

de Bono, E. (2010). *Teach yourself to think*. New York: Penguin Books.

Drucker, P. F. (2008, reissue). *The essential Drucker: The best of sixty years of Peter Drucker's essential writings on management*. New York: HarperBusiness.

Dunbar, R. (1998). *Grooming, gossip and the evolution of language*. Cambridge, MA: Harvard Business Press.

Ericsson, K. A. (1996). *The road to excellence: Acquisition of expert performance in the arts and sciences, sports and game*s. Mahwah, NJ: Lawrence Erlbaum.

Ericsson, K. A. (2009). *Development of professional expertise: Toward measurement of expert performance and design of optimal learning environments*. New York: Cambridge University Press.

Gardner, H. (2011). *Frames of mind: The theory of multiple intelligences*. New York: Basic Books.

Gourville, J. T. (2006, June). Eager sellers and stony buyers: Understanding the psychology of new-product adoption. Harvard Business Review, *84*(6).

Granovetter, M. S. (1973, May). The strength of weak ties. *American Journal of Sociology, 78*(6).

Kirkpatrick, D. L., & Kirkpatrick, J. D. (2006). *Evaluating training programs: The four levels* (3rd ed.). San Francisco, CA: Berrett-Koehler.

Lyall, S. (2009, July 31). No apologies from the boss of a no-frills airline. *New York Times*.

Magretta, J. (2011). *Understanding Michael Porter*. Cambridge, MA: Harvard Business School Press.

Marrow, A. (1970). *The practical theorist: The life and work of Kurt Lewin*. New York: Basic Books.

Mintzberg, H., Ahlstrand, B., & Lampel, J. (2010). *Management—It's not what you think*. Upper Saddle River, NJ: Pearson.

Phillips, J. J. (2003). *Return on investment in training and performance improvement programs* (2nd rev. ed.). Burlington, MA: Butterworth-Heinemann Ltd.

Pink, D. H. (2008). *A whole new mind*. London: Cyan Books.

Raynor, M. E., Ahmed, M., & Henderson, A. D. (2009, April). Are "great" companies just lucky? *Harvard Business Review.*

Seligman, M. (2006). *Learned optimism.* New York: Vintage Books.

Trompenaars, F., Hampden-Turner, C., & Brealey, N. (2012). *Riding the waves of culture.* New York: McGraw-Hill.

Wagner, R. (2006). *12: The elements of great managing.* Washington, DC: Gallup Press.

Index

Announcing the Business Expert Press Digital Library

Concise E-books Business Students Need for Classroom and Research

This book can also be purchased in an e-book collection by your library as
- a one-time purchase,
- that is owned forever,
- allows for simultaneous readers,
- has no restrictions on printing, and
- can be downloaded as PDFs from within the library community.

Our digital library collections are a great solution to beat the rising cost of textbooks. e-books can be loaded into their course management systems or onto student's e-book readers.

The **Business Expert Press** digital libraries are very affordable, with no obligation to buy in future years. For more information, please visit **www.businessexpertpress.com/librarians**. To set up a trial in the United States, please contact **Adam Chesler** at *adam.chesler@businessexpertpress .com* for all other regions, contact **Nicole Lee** at *nicole.lee@igroupnet.com*.

www.ingramcontent.com/pod-product-compliance
Lightning Source LLC
Chambersburg PA
CBHW060544210326
41519CB00014B/3338